Sarah Fell Keppler's

SCHOOL

OF

 *FISH*

A COMPREHENSIVE GUIDE TO KEEPING FRESHWATER TROPICAL FISH

Printed in the United States of America
Library of Congress Catalog Card Number: 90-61224
ISBN 0-9626166-4-8

The author welcomes information and feedback from readers. You can write to her care of the publisher.

Published and distributed by: PETSPUBS PRESS INC
Box 2658
South Hamilton, MA 01982

The information in this book is accurate to the best of the author's knowledge; however, neither the author nor the publisher accepts responsibility for adverse experience. To human intervention, a reluctant Mother Nature yields only partially—and, on occasion, unpredictably.

PERSPECTIVE:

Sarah Fell Keppler comes to her expertise through years of front line, wet-hands experience. Being neither scientist nor academician, she approaches her subject as a practitioner. For over 15 years she has worked in pet shops and taught fishkeeping to new aquarium owners. In this face-to-face, real world involvement, she has experimented, observed and documented. She calls her book a "collaboration"— because it stems from the contributions of *thousands* and *thousands* and *thousands* of beautiful tropical *unsel*fish fish.

The book's approach stems from the author's recognition that the prime purpose of an aquarium is to keep its inhabitants alive! Accomplishing this, therefore, becomes the thrust and emphasis of her book. Sarah Fell Keppler is a different kind of teacher. She understands what background knowledge is key and how to simplify its presentation.

Her technique entails explaining the biological and chemical relationships which underlie aquarium health and proceeding from that understanding to develop the logic of fishkeeping. It is unlike other "fish" books and refreshingly individualistic in selection of subjects, organization of content and manner of presenting its insights.

This is a *must* book for the caring aquarist. The book is intended for all who are interested in freshwater tropical fish:

The beginning hobbyist who does not yet realize what basic knowledge is essential to successful enjoyment.

The practicing aquarist who is frustrated by costs and problems that defy solution.

Those considering aquariums who need an over-all understanding of what owning will entail.

The guide is packed with useful, pertinent, and practical information. Pleasingly novel in content, in organization, in presentation and in style, it gently leads the reader through tightly organized and carefully selected subjects. And, here and there, it "sugar-coats" the learning with a bit of irreverence and occasional asides. It's a teacher with a twinkle in its eye.

Her book helps to keep the hobby fun!

TABLE OF CONTENTS

INTRODUCTION

Hi!

I'm Sarah.

Introduction? . . . How's that for an introduction?

Although my name really is Sarah, to many pet shop customers I am also "the fish lady". I have been working in pet shops, breeding and raising freshwater tropical fish and taking care of aquariums for the last 15 years. Face-to- face, I have taught thousands of people how to care for their fish. I have personally set up hundreds of aquariums and given guidance on many hundreds more. Now, in *School of Fish*, I'm putting in writing what I have been telling people for years.

In talking to all these aquarium owners, I long ago came to realize that I was reciting certain "words of wisdom" again and again. Many new aquarium owners had similar experiences, bumped up against similar dilemmas, and found similar gaps in the information available to them. Eventually, I concluded that a need existed for a "how-to" manual that took into account four of my "pet" convictions:

  1) Small aquariums, from desktop through 55 gallons, are not as forgiving as the very large ones. These smaller ones are "picky", and owners of smaller aquariums experience unnecessary problems because many books give "large aquarium" advice.

  2) Much waste of time and money could be avoided if owners had just a little more understanding of basic fish tank biology.

  3) Fish owners could avoid costly mistakes and buy fish more wisely if they had access to better, and better organized, information about the characteristics and peculiarities of various fish.

  4) Every owner should have access to instructions on how to "cure" a "sick" aquarium.

This book, I think, offers much information that has either been lacking or, at best, hard to find. If you are the owner of - or, if you are considering becoming the owner of - a freshwater, tropical fish aquarium 55 gallons or smaller, this book is for you. This book will tell you what you should know about keeping live fish healthy and happy in a tank. My suggestions and advice come with no guarantees; they stem from my own experiences, observations, successes and failures. I prescribe procedures which will work in smaller tanks . .

. with predictable consistency . . . under what I have found to be typical circumstances. Since I cannot be familiar with your tank or your specific situation, I try always to offer conservative recommendations not likely to cause serious problems even though individual tanks and fish populations differ widely.

Chapters 1 through 4 provide background understanding - information *every* aquarist should have, whether beginner or long time hobbyist. Here I, also, address in detail the subjects which most frequently trouble my customers. I neither gloss over nor ignore important information simply because it happens to be a bit technical. My attempt is to present rather complicated matters in ways that are readily understandable to non-scientific readers. In these chapters I use explanations that have "worked" successfully for me in stores for years.

Aquariums exist *to keep fish alive*! Chapters 5 through 8 describe your enemies and tell you how to recognize them, how to avoid them, and how to eliminate them. I tell you about the critical first weeks with a new tank and the precautions needed. I tell you how to transfer new fish into an aquarium (acclimation) in a manner that reduces the health risk to the existing population and to the newcomers. I describe common health problems and their treatment. Chapter 9 is devoted strictly to those difficult, very small mini- tanks called "desktop" tanks.

Chapter 10 is unique. It's called *The Fishbuyer's Fishfinder*. It is a chronicling of the in-tank compatibility characteristics of 100 different fish. My purpose is to help you make prudent fish selections when bringing new residents to your community. I've tried to anticipate the circumstances under which you might need compatibility information, and I've provided cross references of several different types. I have also included suggested fish groupings which will provide tank color and excitement along with minimum loss of life.

The book closes with a detailed reference index that I call the "Indossary". It is an index - but one with an added feature of serving as a sort of aquarium-word glossary for selected words and terms used in this book.

My goal in writing this book is to give you necessary knowledge in an easy-to-read format. Here and there, to "soften" a book full of "hard" information, I try to interject a little banter or a bit of whimsy. I want this book to be "reader-friendly". I also want it to be a *different and more useful kind* of fish book.

So . . put on your underwater goggles, take a deep breath . . . and here we go.

Chapter 1

THE OTHER SIDE OF THE GLASS

How fish affect waters

How waters affect fish

The food chain

The nitrification cycle

The critical first weeks

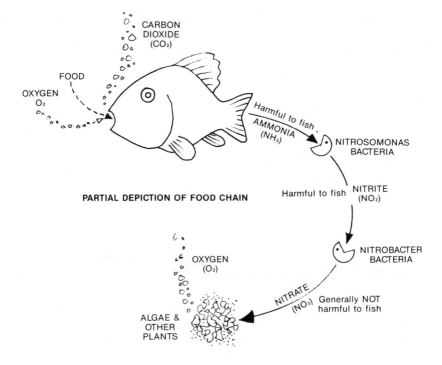

PARTIAL DEPICTION OF FOOD CHAIN

Easy, now . . don't let "The Big Picture" scare you off! Don't be thinking, *Oh my! Only Chapter one and I'm under water already.*

I realize that you didn't ask to become an environmental

engineer. You just want to keep your beautiful fish healthy. Well, fear not. You don't have to memorize the names or the chemical formulas or even who eats what. Those guys up there in the picture are your friends. You know the big guy. Let me introduce the others. You'll be glad you've met them. Trust me!

So, hang in there. I am certain you will find it useful from time to time to take a quick glance at this diagram. To be a successful aquarist you really must have at least some awareness of what is going on in this sketch. Just a general familiarity will give you a much better understanding of what you read about tropical fish and all that you see going on in your aquarium.

Once again, *the fundamental purpose of an aquarium is to keep fish alive*! You are interested in keeping fish alive or you wouldn't have an aquarium; so, don't ignore this chapter. It may save your fishes' life.

There is an "easy" way and a "hard" way to keep an aquarium. Unfortunately, the "hard" way is the way most new hobbyists seem to do it; I call it "hard" because they lose many costly fish and suffer much frustration along the way. They experience problems which would not have arisen had they had a better understanding of *how* an aquarium keeps fish alive.

What's going on in there?

In water everywhere there are bacteria in at least minimal concentrations. Many kinds of bacteria exist, and they feed on different substances. When conditions are right for a specific kind of bacteria, that bacteria type will tend to breed and multiply as long as its increasing numbers can find adequate nourishment in the water. So, an increasing food supply tends to generate more and more of the kind of bacteria that consumes that kind of food.

As the diagram above shows, the fishes eat food, digest it, and the unutilized remains which they excrete into the water becomes **ammonia**. Ammonia can be toxic to fish. The greater the number of fish, the more ammonia that goes into the tank. As the ammonia in the water increases, the number of ammonia-eating bacteria (*Nitrosomonas* bacteria) also increases (if other conditions are right for their growth). The several kinds of bacteria pictured in this diagram are all "aerobic" bacteria, which means that to stay alive they require oxygen in addition to their food.

The waste excreted by the ammonia-eating bacteria is **nitrite**, which also can be toxic to fish. An increase in ammonia-eating bacteria will thus create more nitrite in the water. Nitrite is the food source for a different kind of bacteria (*Nitrobacter* bacteria). As

10

nitrite becomes more plentiful, over time a larger colony of this nitrite-eating bacteria will also grow. And so it goes . . .

The inside of your fish tank is a closed environment - a tiny world all its own. In such an environment, new additions to the tank of any kind - animal, vegetable, chemical, or whatever, will cause changes in that environment. A useful and cautious way to think about this closed environment is to expect that anything added to it will in some manner excrete a "waste" of some sort.

So, *your fish tank is an ecological system which is very susceptible to change.* When one change occurs, others are likely to follow. You, yourself, will be the direct cause of many of the changes - such as adding fish, or removing fish, or failing to change water, or neglecting to correct other environmental conditions which may be deteriorating. Changes of water are especially important and, if improperly handled, can destroy the bacteria colonies which are essential to maintaining the ecological balance. Changes in heat or light or oxygen supply can also be harmful and destructive.

There's a lot going on in that tank - even if you can't see it happening. This book will tell you how to be in charge - how to be the "Big Fish" in this little "pond".

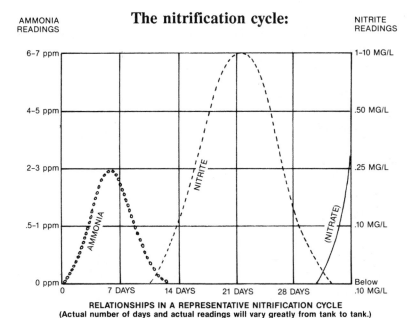

The nitrification cycle:

RELATIONSHIPS IN A REPRESENTATIVE NITRIFICATION CYCLE
(Actual number of days and actual readings will vary greatly from tank to tank.)

OK, OK . . Last time; I won't do it again. I promise. But this chart, too, is essential background information.

These wavy lines are well worth a few minutes of your time. Bear with me, as we go-over the waves.

Along the bottom of the graph, going from left to right you will see that you are moving forward in time . . days, actually. As you move from the bottom of the chart in an upward direction you are reading representative chemical concentrations - the higher on the chart, the greater the amount of that chemical in the water.

The rise and fall of ammonia is indicated by the first curve at the left side of the chart. Representative concentration levels - as determined by test kits available in pet shops - are indicated on the ammonia scale running up the left hand side of the chart. These ammonia concentration levels are measured in parts per million (ppm).

The rise and fall of nitrite concentration is indicated by the dashed line curve in the middle of the chart. Representative test kit readings are shown on the nitrite scale at the extreme right. These **nitrite** concentration levels are measured in milligrams per liter (mg/l).

(**Nitrate** concentration, which is usually not harmful to the fishes - can be seen rising at the end of the cycle and is shown by the solid line at the extreme right.)

Start at the lower left-hand corner of the graph. This point represents the time at which you introduce the first group of fish to an aquarium tank. Directing your eyes to the right, you see that during the next few weeks the chemical make-up of the tank changes greatly.

During the first days in the new tank the fish are consuming food and digesting it, and releasing **ammonia**. The ammonia level in the tank builds up rapidly. Because bacteria increase as their food supply expands - those bacteria which use ammonia as food will increase in number to meet the increasing ammonia level. They will consume the ammonia, convert it and excrete it as **nitrite**. As a result, next comes a rapid decrease in ammonia and an increase in nitrite. In turn, the availability of more nitrite causes an increase in the kind of bacteria that use nitrite for food. The nitrite-eating bacteria convert nitrite to **nitrate**, and soon nitrate replaces nitrite. Unlike the harmful ammonia and **nitrite, nitrate** is harmless to the fish (except in much higher concentrations than likely to occur in even a marginally maintained aquarium). **Nitrate** promotes plant growth (including algae growth) and is basically a fertilizer.

You have just stepped your way through the *Nitrification Cycle* or Nitrogen Cycle. It occurs in a tank newly stocked with fish or in one that you have emptied and started over. It occurs while the initial bacteria colonies are becoming established and the tank is cycling to conditions of stability.

Inexpensive water testing kits available at pet shops allow you to determine the chemical concentrations in a tank. By comparing how your own measurements change with the diagram above you will be able to make judgments about progress through the nitrification cycle. Similarly, you can also determine when something is not behaving according to normal expectations and is therefore out of control.

The number of weeks shown on the chart are only approximate, or representative, times. Tanks with differing fish and differing filters will cycle in differing numbers of weeks. Not all tanks will cycle in 4 weeks; some will take twice as long. 4 to 6 weeks duration is quite commonly experienced.

Number of fish at the outset:

This *Nitrification Cycle* - the initial building up of the "good" bacteria colony - can only occur if the fish population in the tank remains stable throughout the several cycling weeks. Also, if there are too many fish in the cycling group for either the tank size or its filtration capacity, the nitrification cycle will not play out as the chart shows. Biological stability will not be attained. Below is a table suggesting the *maximum* number of fish to use as a starting, or "cycling", population. The size of the fish selected sets the limit on the number. With smaller fish a greater number are acceptable. For this reason, the table describes the limitations in total *inches of fish*. To determine total "inches of fish" measure the body length of each fish - *not including the tail*, and add these together. (Estimates will have to do; getting the fish to stand still for measurement is beyond the scope of this book.)

Tank Size	Inches of Fish
5 gallons	3 inches
10 gallons	6 inches
15 gallons	7 inches
20 gallons	8 inches
25 gallons	9 inches
29/30 gallons	10 inches
45 gallons	13 inches
55 gallons	15 inches

Procedure:

Place *all* of the fish you select for the cycling population into the tank. *Do not add any fish while the tank is still progressing through the nitrification cycle.* During the cycling period, feed the fish lightly - about 2 flakes of fish food for each "inch of fish", once a day.

Effect of adding fish later:

The several week nitrification cycle essentially occurs only during a tank start-up or start-over. After the tank has successfully completed the nitrification cycle, adding to the number of fish in the tank will cause changes in the chemical concentrations; but, the rise and fall of the ammonia and nitrite will occur quickly, and the tank should reach stability within a few hours. **Caution:** this will only be true *if:* (1) the total fish population remains within the capacity of the filter installation, (2) the total fish inches of each addition to the tank are *no greater* (and preferably less) than the total inches in the original cycling population, and (3) additions are made no more frequently than a week apart.

Congratulations!

If you have gained at least a general understanding of the material in this chapter, you are now a fairly sophisticated fish-keeper and you are already a graduate student in "School of Fish". That wasn't so hard, was it?

Chapter 2

DR. GOODTANK

6 goals of tank-keeping

Oxygen

Ammonia

pH

Mother Nature has a harder time reaching inside a tank, so it's up to you to look out for those pretty fishes. *You* become their benefactor and protector. One might say that they look up to you. But, then you knew that, didn't you?

You are going to provide food, see that the tank has an adequate supply of oxygen, and protect your fish from all harmful forms of pollution and disease. Easy to say, but what does that entail? I think it will be helpful to take a sort of over-all look at just what we are trying to accomplish in managing our aquaria.

Described below are the six environmental factors that are key to operating a safe and healthy aquarium. On a regular basis you should be monitoring and controlling these variable conditions. Mastery of these six factors is what I think aquarium management is all about for most freshwater tropical fish owners.

1. Keep the water in continuous **circulation**.

   Why? For two reasons:

   a) In order to stay alive fish must extract **oxygen** from the water by taking in water through their mouths and passing it over their gills. The gills separate and remove oxygen from water. Such oxygen in the water is called, "absorbed oxygen" because it has been absorbed by the water after being trapped in the water. It is also called "dissolved oxygen". Since the water renews its oxygen supply chiefly at its surface, we want to force as much water as possible to the surface and into contact with the atmosphere as frequently as possible.

b) We want to force as much water as possible to flow through the filter media so effective filtering can take place continuously and also so the bacteria colonies which live in the filter media receive the continuous oxygen supply they require.

How? By creating flow - typically, either through the introduction of a continuously rising column of bubbles, or by drawing water through a motor- driven, impeller pump and discharging it under pressure back to the tank. (Chapter 3 describes circulation and aeration in detail.)

2. Maintain **turbulent** conditions at the water's surface.

Why? Water entraps air at its surface and then absorbs oxygen from the entrapped air. An excited and turbulent surface entraps more air than a calm surface.

How? By arranging to discharge re-circulated water at the surface in a manner that agitates the surface and, in many tanks, by the continuing collapse of bubbles at the surface. (Chapter 3, describes turbulence and bubble columns in detail.)

3. Get rid of the **ammonia** that the fish excrete into the water as the residue from the their consumption of food.

Why? When ammonia levels build up in the water, the water can harm the fish in at least three ways:

a) burning the fishes' gills and thereby reducing the gills' ability to extract needed oxygen from the water.

b) burning the fishes' mucous slime coat (their "skin") which serves as the fishes' protection from attack by parasites in the water.

c) in severe cases, actually burning the flesh of the fishes so severely that ulceration occurs.

Any of these conditions, if serious enough, can be fatal.

How?   By promoting the growth and survival of the kind of bacteria which convert ammonia into **nitrites** and another kind of bacteria which convert the nitrites into harmless **nitrates**. This entails providing an adequate place for the bacteria to adhere and to grow - and delivering a continuous flow of oxygen- laden water to these "oxygen-eating" (aerobic) bacteria. (Chapter 1 discusses these bacteria.)

4. Regulate and control the **temperature** of the water.

Why?   If the water temperature gets *too low*, a fish may start to slough off the mucous slime coat which protects it from parasite infestation. At the other extreme, *high* temperatures sharply reduce the oxygen carrying capacity of the water. I suggest 78 degrees Fahrenheit as a workable target temperature for most aquariums. More important perhaps than the exact temperature is how much the temperature *varies*. In my experience, the fish are not likely to be harmed by temperatures anywhere between 70 and 83 degrees - *provided that the temperature does not vary more than 4 degrees* over a short period of time. Temperature fluctuation causes stress which makes the fish more susceptible to disease and infection.

How?   Pet shops carry a variety of heaters, thermometers and the combination heater/thermostats which control temperature automatically.

5. Maintain the water at desired *pH* level.

(pH is a measure of either alkalinity or acidity. A pH reading of 7 is neutral - neither acid nor alkaline. Numbers below 7 indicate acidity with the lowest number being the most **acid**; numbers above 7 are showing alkalinity, with the highest number being the most **alkaline**.)

Why?   Some tropical fishes prefer acid waters; but, the general rule for *most* tropical fish aquariums is *prevent acidity*. Most tropical fishes will tolerate and normally continue to thrive in moderately **alkaline** waters - even with alkalinity readings up to 8.2 or 8.4. Except for a few fish species, or when special acid conditions are needed for fish breeding, I have found that a little alkalinity is usually not detrimental. (Individual species of fish require differing water conditions for breeding, and many breed best in acid waters.) For tanks not used either for breeding or for fish which prefer acid waters, acidity (pH number below 7) almost always causes biological filtration problems. Acid waters interfere with bacterial action. When the waters are decidedly acid (below 6.8), the bacteria simply do not perform their normal pollution removal functions effectively, and the tank can support only a reduced fish population.

I have long felt that too much emphasis is placed on fine-tuning pH to maintain a constant 7.0 neutrality. My personal experience has been that somewhat alkaline water in a range of 7.0 to 7.8 is usually quite acceptable to the fish.

Breeding is a different matter entirely. When breeding fish, strict maintenance of the best pH for the species is extremely important.

How?   The first requirement is to measure and know the pH of your tap water. If your fish population is adaptable - and, if your tap water is not distinctly acid, operating your tank at a pH level about the same as your local tap water is obviously convenient. (If you use local tap water it must be free of chlorine. Inexpensive dechlorinating chemical additives are described below and are available in the pet shops.) When it does become necessary to adjust the pH of your tank, there are several ways to accomplish it. Depending upon the pH of your tap water in relation to the existing pH in the tank, tap water as replacement for some of the tank water may move the tank pH in the desired direction. (For example, if the tank has an acid pH reading of 6.7 and your tap water has a pH of 7.1, substitution of tap water for some tank water will result in raising the pH of the tank water.) Adding bottled drinking water, which is usually near a neutral 7.0, will dilute and reduce either an acid or alkaline situation. Bottled water, however, is probably too sterile to allow it to become a major portion of the tank water. Treatment with **sodium biphosphate** will lower alkalinity making the water more acid (called *"buffering down"*) while treatment with **sodium bicarbonate** will reduce acidity making the water more alkaline (called *"buffering up"*). If the water remains consistently acid, the addition to the tank of a shell or two (flat shells, so the fish will not get caught in them) can *raise* and keep the pH higher. The addition of plants or pieces of driftwood (pre-sterilized for aquarium use) will slowly *lower* pH. Even a small build up of detritus (debris) on the filter media also "buffers down" the pH.

6. Keep the water **clear**.

Why?   Obviously you need relatively clear water so you can see and better enjoy watching your fish. Although crystal clear water is the personal ambition of many hobbyists, this is less important than maintaining a balanced ecology in the aquarium to keep the fish alive. An aquarium with a balanced ecology will always have clear water, but it will not always be crystal clear. Water becomes cloudy either because more food is going into the water than the fish need or because floating bacteria do not have adequate or suitable surfaces for anchoring and colonizing.

How?   By not over-feeding (putting more food in the water than the fish eat quickly) and by providing mechanical filtering devices and circulating the water through them to entrap both visible and microscopic particles which are floating in the water.

So, above are six considerations to check off mentally each time you look at your tank and think, *"How are my fish?"* and, *"Am I treating them right?"*. Your fish will be relieved and pleased to know an owner has their water on the brain.

Chapter 3

HOW THE WATER WORKS

Aeration

Circulation

Turbulence

A bubble factory! Isn't that what the aquarium section of a large pet shop looks like? There has to be a market for bubbles somewhere; otherwise, why would this place manufacture so many?

There's nothing new to understand about bubbles, right? Well, maybe yes, maybe no. Why those tanks are full of bubbles may not be quite so obvious. Did you think the bubbles were there for the fish to breathe? You don't see fish snapping at the bubbles though, do you? You know why? Because those are *air* bubbles and fish don't inhale air; they gulp *water*, pass the water over their gills, and the gills extract **dissolved oxygen** from the water. The gills then expel carbon dioxide into the water.

Okay, so if fish don't breathe the bubbles, why the bubbles? Well, first lets look at some of the peculiarities of bubbles. A gas - any gas, generated or released within a body of water, forms bubbles. Since gases are lighter in weight than water, the bubbles rise to the surface of the water. As the bubbles rise they expand in size because the water pressure exerted on the bubbles becomes less and less as the water around them becomes more shallow. The bubbles continue to expand as they rise until they reach the water surface. When the bubbles break the surface and join the atmosphere they collapse violently as water rushes in to fill the void caused by the collapse. When many bubbles collapse in rapid succession the water around the collapsing bubbles becomes agitated and turbulent.

Turbulence is a key word. When surface conditions are turbulent, little globules of air become trapped in the water. This entrapped air provides the **oxygen** which dissolves in the water. The bubbles themselves, you remember, were formed from air pumped into the tank; and, the bubbles didn't stay in the water; they escaped at the surface. So, collapsing air bubbles produce turbulence;

turbulent waters ensnare air globules; air globules contain the oxygen which dissolves in the water; and, fish gills extract dissolved oxygen from the water.

In addition to collapsing on the surface, there is a second way that bubbles help to produce surface turbulence. If rising gas bubbles are forced to rise in a restricted path such as a vertical tube placed in the tank - and if that tube is open at the bottom, the rising bubbles will initiate an upward flow of water in the tube. Water flowing upward in the tube draws replacement water from the tank bottom, and water in the tank begins to circulate. If the upward current in the tube is allowed to spill out onto the surface in a manner that imparts a directional flow, Bingo - a jet of water shoots onto the surface, and agitates the water and creates - you guessed it - more powerful surface **turbulence**! More turbulence allows the water to entrap more air.

Getting air into the water is called **aeration**. Surface contact with the atmosphere is the chief way of aerating the water. Aerated water supplies dissolved oxygen not only to the fishes but also to the aerobic bacteria colonies. (If there is plant life in the tank, the plants will give off some additional oxygen into the water.)

So much for bubbles and how to use them to affect oxygen supply. We previously described how a rising column of bubbles can create **water circulation**. Circulation itself is vitally important for at least two reasons: 1) to keep bringing "stale" water up to the surface where it is re- aerated and where the carbon dioxide escapes, and 2) to cause *all* the water in the aquarium to flow periodically through whatever filter media is in use so the media will cleanse the water of harmful impurities and so the aerobic bacteria colonies anchored to the media will receive their needed oxygen.

Bubbles aren't the only way to force **water circulation** in a tank, and they aren't the only method of causing **surface turbulence**. Remember the resemblance to a bubble factory? Well, once the bubble fascination passes, a visitor might notice that not all the aquariums show bubbles - yet their fish residents still seem healthy and happy. Aha! You don't absolutely need bubbles! There are obviously other ways to cause **surface turbulence and circulation** - without bubbles. Electric motor driven impeller pumps are very frequently employed to shoot a stream of water from the bottom to the surface - and they too keep the water in circulation. Jets of water shooting under the surface can also create circulation.

What about an aquarium that has no visible surface agitation or turbulence - no bubbles or jet streams? Will all the fish and "good" bacteria die?

There is a certain amount of circulation and aeration continuously going on in any tank even though that circulation may not be visible. Uneven heating from the sun or electric light or an electric heater will cause warmer water to rise and create circulation; invisible rising bubbles of carbon dioxide given off by the fishes and oxygen given off by plants produce minor circulation; fishes breaking the water surface stimulate the waters. A continuing exchange of gases (aeration) goes on at the water's surface even in relatively still water. So it is conceivable that a balanced aquarium under ideal conditions would support its population without artificially stimulated circulation and turbulence. Ideal conditions would involve the relationship between surface area, number and kinds of fishes, selection of plants, light and heat, as well as other factors. Lacking such ideal conditions, some contrived method of stimulating circulation brings more of the water into contact with the surface faster and more frequently. This insures continuing, ample aeration and frequent recirculation through the filters.

Anyhow - back to bubbles. Bubbles are not the *only way* to agitate and circulate - maybe not even the best way - but they are *one way* and probably the prettiest way - and anyway I wanted to address this bubble thing.

Okay . . . so I made a big deal about bubbles!

Chapter 4

AT THE WATERWORKS

> What filtration is
>
> Kinds of filtration
>
> Classification of filters
>
> Filter & tank maintenance
>
> Algae

You can't wash water . . and if you could, how would you dry it? **Filtration** is how we clean water in the aquarium.

Kinds of filtration:

Most of us have had experience with one or another sort of filter. We probably most frequently think of a filter as a device which allows air or fluid to pass but blocks and entraps any particles. Most of us, at one time or another, have had to clean or replace such a filter when it became clogged.

There are filters in aquariums which do that same kind of filtering - remove particles, both visible and microscopic in size. This is **MECHANICAL** filtration (or, particulate filtration). Mechanical filtration is required in all aquariums, however, it is not the only filtration process used in aquariums. The most important to fish life is **BIOLOGICAL** filtration, which consists of growing and maintaining colonies of living organisms (bacteria) to consume the harmful ammonia and nitrite toxins. Finally, **CHEMICAL** filtration is a third kind often used in aquariums. Although most aquariums can get along without it, chemical filtration not only assists in purification, but often will prevent the yellowish cast that older water sometimes takes on. Proper chemical filtration "polishes" water - which means that it makes the water clear or clearer. Chemical filtration entails putting into the tank certain chemically active materials which will absorb harmful organic and inorganic compounds, some metals and some gasses. Commonly used substances for chemical filtering include carbon, zeolite and other ion exchange resins.

Why filter?

Remember, an aquarium is a closed environment - a mini-ecology system. As would be true with people or animals or any living organisms, when a large population is confined to a small enclosure or compound, waste removal becomes essential. Without waste removal, the fish would eventually die of disease or toxicity. Both ammonia and nitrite come from fish waste, and both are toxic to the fishes.

The most important reason to filter aquarium water is to protect fish health. Water is also filtered for the secondary purpose of removing visible debris to prevent the water from becoming cloudy or murky. Clear water makes the fish more visible and the viewing more fun.

Biological filtration:

BIOLOGICAL is the kind of filtration most critical to health of your fish. (It is also called bacteriological filtration.) It should be in every aquarium. When fish waste enters the water it becomes **ammonia**. Biological filters are designed to become a home for two kinds of bacteria colonies. The first (nitrosomonas bacteria) consume ammonia ($NH3$) and excrete **nitrite** ($NO2$); the second (nitrobacter bacteria) consume the nitrite and give off **nitrate** ($NO3$). If nitrites and ammonia were not consumed and were allowed to accumulate the fish would quickly die. So, BIOLOGICAL filters provide a suitable place for "good" bacteria to adhere (colonize) and to grow. The filter's circulation system then causes the water to circulate continuously through these colonies providing the bacteria with the oxygen they require. Almost no aquarium supports fish life for long without adequate biological filtration.

An adequate BIOLOGICAL filter system provides ample surface area for anchoring and growing large enough bacteria colonies to consume the amount of waste generated. To be adequate, a system must also deliver to the bacteria a sufficient, continuous flow of water rich in oxygen.

Bacteria colonies build up gradually - over a period of weeks. Once established, bacteria colonies are vulnerable to depletion and destruction. Cleaning the filters - removing collected particles from filter media, must be done carefully with the least disruption possible of existing bacteria colonies. Also to prevent radical changes in existing water chemistry, during routine water changes replace only

1/4 to 1/3 of the tank water - *never all the water.*

Filters in general:

Aquarium shops display a wide variety of filter equipment and filtration devices. Regardless of how these differ in appearance, each performs *one or more* of the three types of filtration just discussed: BIOLOGICAL (Bacteriological), MECHANICAL (Particle), or CHEMICAL. Some filters are designed to do two or all three of the types of filtration; however, multipurpose filters often do one type of filtration well and other types not as effectively. Costs of filters span a wide range. This chapter will take a look at the more common kinds of filter systems but will examine in detail only undergravel filters.

All filters - no matter which kind of filtration performed or what filter media employed - have one requirement in common. To function well the system must cause a large portion of the aquarium water to *circulate* through whatever filter **media** it provides. Filter systems create such circulation either with rising columns of air bubbles or with impeller type circulating pumps driven by small electric motors.

Different filter designs employ a wide variety of materials for filter **media**. Among the arrangements used are beds of gravel, other types of granular material, layers of woven floss, sponges, activated carbon cartridges, cartridges containing ion exchange resins, and assemblies of these and other materials in combination with each other.

Some filter designs place the filter media *inside* the main aquarium tank while others draw the aquarium water *out of the tank* for filtering. Those that draw water outside circulate it through an external water box containing the filtering media and return it to the tank.

Classifications of filters:

The packaged filters offered for sale in stores usually describe the filter as one of the following:

      1. Undergravel Filter (media in aquarium)
      2. Sponge filter (media in aquarium)
      3. Box filter (media inside aquarium)
      4. Canister filter (media outside aquarium)
      5. Outside filter (media outside aquarium)
      6. Wet/Dry filter

Power Filter is a name sometimes also used for any filter - regardless of type - which has its media *outside* the aquarium and therefore relies upon an electric motor driven impeller pump to circulate water.

The undergravel filter:

Because knowledge of an undergravel filter's functioning is basic to understanding aquariums, this chapter will describe its workings in detail. If you understand how undergravel filters perform, you will not find it difficult to figure out the other common types because their workings are somewhat more obvious and more easily understood.

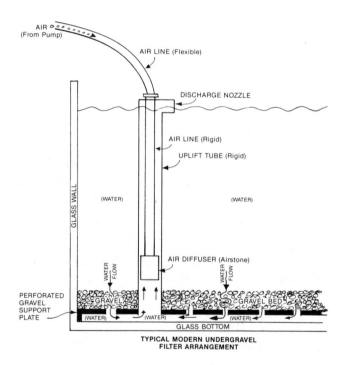

TYPICAL MODERN UNDERGRAVEL
FILTER ARRANGEMENT

An UNDERGRAVEL FILTER employs a bed of "gravel" near the bottom of the aquarium to remove and capture foreign particles from circulating aquarium water. The bed of gravel lies on a rigid plastic piece called a gravel **support plate**. The support plate elevates the bed slightly above the aquarium floor. Perforations in the support plate permit water to flow through the plate and through the gravel bed it supports. The plate perforations are too small to allow the gravel pieces to fall through. Since the plate holds the gravel above the aquarium floor there is water space underneath the gravel bed; thus, water is above, under, and in the bed. The beneficial bacteria adhere to the surfaces of all the individual pieces of gravel.

An undergravel filter system incorporates one or more vertical tubes (usually at least two) which allow water to flow upward from underneath the gravel bed directly to the top surface of the aquarium. Typically, rigid plastic tubes (water **uplift tubes**) fit in holes in the support plate. The bottom of the uplift tubes passes through both the gravel bed and the support plate. The upper end of the tubes is at the water surface. Air, pumped from outside the tank, flows through plastic tubing (**air lines**) which ends at the lower end of each uplift tube. The air then proceeds to bubble upward through each uplift tube. The rising bubbles cause an upward column of water to flow in the tube. The upward circulation of water in the tube pulls replacement water downward through the gravel bed to the space below the plate and then into the tube to chase and replace water moving up the tube. This sets up a current which continuously pulls water downward through the gravel bed for filtering.

It is on and in the gravel bed that both the removal of floating particles (MECHANICAL filtration) and the growth of "good" bacteria (BIOLOGICAL filtration) occurs. The gravel prevents waste and foreign particles from passage. These then collect on the top surface of the bed and within the bed. The aerobic bacteria anchor to the gravel surfaces where circulating water continuously brings to them their needed supply of fresh oxygen.

Removal of particles (mechanical filtration) begins as soon as water circulation starts through the bed in response to the introduction of the air bubbles. Biological filtration, because it requires "good" bacteria colonies in place, cannot start until an adequate colony of bacteria builds up. In a new tank this process typically requires from 4 to 6 weeks so long as the original, small cycling population of fish in the tank is neither increased nor decreased during this period. (During this period of building bacteria colonies, the tank is progressing through the nitrification cycle previously described in Chapter 1.)

The quantity of aerobic bacteria required to consume ammonia and nitrite and to maintain the tank's biological stability depends, of course, upon how much fish waste must be consumed. The amount to be consumed, in turn, depends upon the number of fish, their size and how much they are fed. The filtering system can only grow as much bacteria as its total gravel surface and oxygen delivery capability permits. So, there is always a danger of having an installed filter system which is inadequate in capacity - not enough gravel or too little oxygen.

As a rule of thumb, I suggest the following amounts of gravel to achieve optimum performance from an undergravel filter:

Tank Size	Gravel
10 gallons	15 lbs.
20 gallons (high)	30 lbs.
20 gallons (long)	35 lbs.
29 gallons	40 lbs.
30 gallons	45 lbs.
55 gallons	70-80 lbs.

Most of the newer undergravel filter designs include provision for also incorporating chemical filtration by insertion of a carbon or zeolite cartridge. The cartridge slides into the top discharge section of the uplift tube. The cartridges last only about three weeks and should then be replaced. If at that time continued chemical filtration is no longer desired, remove and discard the spent cartridges.

Other kinds of filters:

I will discuss other kinds of filters only briefly. Manufacturers' individual designs vary greatly. With an understanding of undergravel filters and some general information about other common types, you will be able to understand other filters from the manufacturers' descriptions on the packages.

In **Sponge Filters** a sponge performs the mechanical filtration. The pores of the sponge also become the surfaces upon which the bacteria colonies adhere. When using sponge filters in a larger tank (20 gallons or more) it is often advisable to use at least two to create enough current for good aeration.

Box Filters feature a containment box lightly packed with woven floss and a layer of activated carbon or activated carbon and zeolite. This type of filter requires frequent changes of filter material. The frequent changes destroy most of the bacteria colonies. For this reason I do not consider box filters used alone as adequate biological filtration.

Canister Filters contain one or more compartments through which circulating aquarium water is forced to flow. Some of the more common types feature a compartment containing ceramic "bio-noodles" and another compartment containing woven floss with carbon, zeolite, or carbon-like materials.

Outside Filters incorporate a disposable cartridge housed in a plastic box which hangs on the outside of the tank. The cartridge holds a woven floss bag containing porous carbon filter media or some other media material such as a small sponge. Water is pumped through the cartridge and back to the tank.

Wet/Dry Filters are biological filters with a mechanical pre-filter. Wet/Dry filters are complicated, high-technology devices capable of sustaining small living reefs. While remarkable systems, they are so costly that they are beyond the reach of most hobbyists.

Selection of kinds of filters for your tank:

Opinions differ about what kinds of filters to use with differing tank set-ups and tank populations. There are no firm rules and no universal answers. The size of your tank has something to do with it. How much you are willing to pay is a major consideration. All six kinds of filters perform MECHANICAL filtration. As stated earlier, your first concern should be to select a system that will perform adequate BIOLOGICAL filtration. Almost any filter system can lay claim to some measure of biological filtration because water containing oxygen is circulated and some sort of filter media is provided upon which at least some "good" bacteria will grow. For this reason, any of the first five types mentioned above can legitimately claim to provide at least a degree of biological filtration. In my judgment, however, the frequent replacement or cleaning of filter media needed in **Box Filters** and **Outside Filters** makes it very difficult to maintain a stable bacteria colony. Each cleaning or replacement results in the destruction of some of the existing bacteria colony. I therefore suggest selecting either an **Undergravel Filter** or a **Sponge Filter** as your primary biological filter. I use **Box** and **Outside** filters as secondary or auxiliary filters only.

Although I prefer to use **Canister Filters** also as auxiliary filters, one of good design can serve alone as a primary filter. (As a secondary to an under-gravel, a canister filter is an excellent addition and provides expanded biological filtration and increased aeration as well as chemical filtration and purification.)

Outside Filters often incorporate a carbon cartridge, or sometimes a zeolite cartridge. This increases the capacity for absorbing ammonia and is an especially desirable auxiliary filter in high ammonia tanks. Goldfish, for example, create a particularly difficult ammonia problem, and often the addition of a carbon or zeolite packed **Box Filter** greatly improves ammonia removal.

Filter and tank maintenance:

Let's start the subject of maintenance with a few general observations about all aquariums and all filtering mechanisms:

1. All require periodic maintenance - checking and servicing of one sort or another.

2. Reduced air flow and *air flow blockage* are common problems often caused by mineral deposits at those surfaces which are in contact with both air and water at the same time. Changing, cleaning or reaming air lines and air devices usually will reinstate flow. Airstones, however, are virtually impossible to clean when they become clogged and should just be thrown away. Sometimes easily removed restrictions or kinks in air lines also interrupt flow.

3. Air pumps frequently fail to deliver the designed amount of air because pump diaphragms or gang valves have failed and need replacement. If all parts are in good working order and the amount of air is still inadequate you probably need a more powerful pump. (Cigarette smoke can cause aquarium air pumps to require frequent internal cleaning because of nicotine resin build-up on the valves.)

4. Many pieces of aquarium equipment have parts that will some time need replacement. Before you purchase equipment, find out whether your pet store regularly stocks all the parts you might have to replace quickly. Examples of such parts are air pump diaphragms, air valves, air filters, motor impellers, and motor impeller magnet assemblies.

5. You can reduce the unsightly problem of *hard water deposits* on aquarium walls by keeping the tank filled as close to the brim as possible. The deposits which accumulate at the line where the air and water meet will thus be hidden under the rim of the tank cover. On glass walled aquaria (not acrylic) mineral deposits can be removed by scraping with a razor

blade, but be careful not to damage the seals which connect the glass panels.

6. All aquariums should have partial water changes every two or three weeks. Replace from 1/4 to 1/3 of the tank water. At water change times the existing bacteria colonies on the biological filter media are at risk. Make changes carefully. On a new tank no water changes or filter maintenance should be done for about 2 to 3 months after introducing the initial, cycling fish population. This is to give the bacteria colonies ample time to become established and effective.

Now for some observations about maintenance as it applies to specific types of filters:

Undergravel filters: During routine water changes, use a siphon type gravel vacuum to clean the gravel. Vacuuming presents an additional risk to the existing bacteria colonies of biological filters. Your pet shop advisor can show you how to vacuum the gravel carefully to avoid, as much as possible, disturbing the bacteria.

Sponge filters: Trapped particles will eventually clog the pores of the sponge and restrict water passage. About every 3 to 4 weeks clear the sponges of these particles. Wring out and rinse the sponge but take care to cause as little reduction as possible in the bacteria growing on the sponge pore's surfaces. If the rinse water contains chlorine, or is not close to the same temperature as the tank, the bacteria may be killed. To minimize harm to the bacteria living on the sponge, rinse the sponge with water taken from the tank during a water change.

Outside filters: Replace the filter media cartridge approximately every 3 weeks because by then, whether or not visible, the pores of the carbon will have become clogged and will no longer absorb. The floss portion of the filter can be rinsed. The carbon portion cannot be rinsed and should be replaced. If the cartridge contains carbon, replace it every 2 to 3 weeks. If it contains zeolite without carbon, the amount of ammonia which must be removed determines the length of time the zeolite will function without recharging or replacement. With high ammonia levels, expect to replace or recharge zeolite in 24 to 48 hours. If a tank has completed cycling and ammonia levels are under control, expect the zeolite to last for 3 weeks or more. Zeolite can be recharged for reuse by soaking for 24 hours in a heavy, non- iodized salt solution.

During the nitrification cycling process, only use **zeolite** if the chemicals become dangerously high because the zeolite, by removing ammonia, will be depriving the bacteria of their food source. Insufficient food would disrupt the process of establishing bacteria colonies.

Tank overheating:

Tank overheating is sometimes difficult to prevent in the summer. If this is happening, first be sure that the tank heater is functioning properly and not coming on when unneeded. If the heater is functioning properly, cool the tank by keeping the lights off and the aquarium cover open to achieve evaporative cooling. An uncovered aquarium risks a fish or two jumping out, but that risk may be preferable to the greater risk of losing the entire population because temperatures are too high. A screen or cheese cloth substitute for the top would be advantageous. Lowering the water level an inch can make it less likely that fish will go over the wall.

Algae:

Cloudy water is generally a sign of a bacterial bloom or an **algae bloom**. A milky color suggests bacterial bloom, and Chapters 7 and 8 address those kinds of problems. (Keep in mind, however, that a possible cause of any excessive bacteria is the inability of the filter to cope with all the waste given off by the fish.) If however the water shows a greenish or brownish cast when drained into a white bucket, the cloudy water is probably caused by algae.

For algae-eating fish, algae are a needed food source. Algae becomes a problem, however, when algae blooms make the water too cloudy, or when excessive brown or green algae build up on aquarium glass, ornaments, plants and gravel. The likely causes of problem algae are either extremely high nutrient (eg: nitrate) level in the water or too much light. Excessive light may result from too much sun or too many hours of aquarium lighting.

Nitrate test kits exist, but they are not readily available in many pet stores. If excessive nitrate is the suspected cause, the nitrate level can be reduced by water changes as described in Chapter 8. If lighting is the cause, reducing the number of lighting hours will reduce the algae; however, you may want to approach the problem also in other ways.

Brown and green algae offer somewhat differing removal problems because algae-eating fish are more effective against the green than the brown. The Chinese Algae Eater offers a possible solution, although it can become aggressive as it grows larger or if it cannot find enough algae to satisfy its hunger. The Plecostomus is perhaps a more desirable tenant but a bit more expensive and somewhat harder to keep alive. Sometimes you can help keep Plecos alive by adding a piece of aquarium-ready (pre-sterilized) driftwood or by providing a diet subsidy. Driftwood will serve as a place for more algae to adhere; and, algae eaters will also eat the wood. (You can read about the Chinese Algae Eater and the Plecostomus in Chapter 10.)

If algae eating fish do not do a satisfactory job because the algae is brown, it is possible to cause algae to turn from brown to green by increasing lighting hours. After the algae turns green, reduce the lighting to less than 12 hours a day but still enough to keep the algae green and attractive to algae-eaters. You can also purchase chemical algicides to remove algae but remember that if algae-eating fish are in the tank, removal of algae reduces or eliminates their food supply.

Exit the waterworks:

Aquarium filtration is a broad subject. In this chapter I have covered the basic and most important aspects as I see them. With this and a little guidance from your pet shop operator, I think you are now equipped to make appropriate filter system choices and to keep your tank in working order. I hope my suggestions, advice and cautions work for you. They have for me.

Chapter 5

SWIM THE FRIENDLY WATERS

Precautions in water mixing

How to add new fish

Acclimation

Fishes, like many humans, do not react well to sudden changes in their environment. Caution and care are the watchwords when you make changes in the water world of the aquarium.

Earlier chapters had much to say about interaction between the fishes and the water they live in. Those chapters described what happens to the water when you first put fish in a tank. They discussed the importance of a stable group of fish during tank cycling. They told about the need to accommodate a large enough colony of bacteria in relation to the size and make-up of the fish population. They explained how to monitor and control water conditions.

From the earlier chapters you are probably already aware that when you remove water from the tank and replace it with new water, or when you move fishes from one container of water to another, you need to be very cautious about how the changes in water will affect the fishes involved. Either *mixing aquarium waters* or *moving fish from one water to another* should be done carefully and in a series of gradual steps. It should be accomplished in ways that do not subject the fish to radical change in temperature, in pH or in other water conditions.

Your own intentional actions often cause the kinds of changes which require the most care. Three common examples are: 1) routine replacement of old aquarium water with new, 2) moving fish from one aquarium to another, and 3) adding newly acquired fish to the aquarium. Typically in these kinds of changes you become involved either with fish in a plastic bag or with fish which have been placed in some other sort of temporary container, such as a bucket. This chapter describes protective methods of handling such situations.

First let's describe *how to add newly acquired fish to an established aquarium*. Since the aquarium's size and filter capacity limit the number of fish it can accommodate, you must first decide that the addition of your new fish will not result in too many fish for your tank. Your next concern is how the change in water environment will affect the new fish. The process of adapting a fish to new waters in a manner that will not harm it or the existing aquarium population is called "**acclimation**".

Newly purchased fishes are usually in a plastic bag. The *acclimation of these new fish* - properly moving them from the bag to the aquarium - involves several precautionary steps. Since the bag contains air as well as water, it will float   To avoid temperature shock on the fishes, float the sealed bag containing the fish on the water in the aquarium for 15 or 20 minutes. This will allow the water in the bag to reach the same temperature as the water in the aquarium.

Having now eliminated the possibility of temperature shock, the next concern is to adjust the new fish gradually to the existing aquarium water pH and other conditions and contaminates. To accomplish this, mix water from the aquarium with the bag water. (Both are now at the same temperature.) Open the bag and add aquarium water in an amount equal to about 1/4 of the original bag contents. Re- seal and re-float the bag to maintain aquarium temperature in the bag and wait 15 to 20 minutes more. If after 15 or 20 minutes the mixed waters in the bag are clear and colorless, empty the bag, fish and all, into the aquarium. If the bag water is not clear or its color suggests that it is no longer clean, do not add it to the aquarium; simply net the fish into the aquarium and throw the bag water away. An even more cautious procedure is to just throw away all bag water whether or not it remains clear. (Although I have generally found it to be unnecessary, repeating the 1/4 water addition a second time would be an added precaution.)

When you find it necessary *to move fish from one aquarium to another* it often involves two environment changes for the fishes. Not only will the fish ultimately be experiencing new aquarium water but also they may have to endure for a time a temporary water change to a bucket or a plastic bag. You should reduce the shock to the fishes by obtaining as much of the temporary container water as possible from the original aquarium.

Although it is seldom desirable to empty completely an established healthy aquarium, if you were to do so the procedures in the preceding paragraph would also apply. In those instances when it becomes necessary to tear-down a tank completely because the water chemistry has deteriorated so badly that any attempt to correct it would be futile, an abrupt change in environment may be unavoidable. Such a change will be highly stressful to the fish and will probably cause losses; but under certain conditions (See Chapter 8), there may be no alternative. In such circumstances it is still desirable to use the "bad" water from the aquarium in any temporary container needed, so that the fish are subjected to only one abrupt environment change. In tear- down situations, also, you should consider attempting to preserve some of the bacteria on the filter media. In the case of gravel, this can be done by removing about 1/20th of the gravel bed, rinse it free of debris with unchlorinated room temperature water, and preserve the remaining bacteria by keeping the gravel dampened with unchlorinated room temperature water. When the aquarium is set-up again, use this gravel to place on top of the new gravel bed to "re- seed" the bed with bacteria.

For smaller fish, it is probably easiest when possible to use plastic bags as temporary containers. If however you are moving fish from a bucket to an established tank, I prefer to remove at least 2/3 of the water in the bucket leaving it about 1/3 full. Then take temperature readings and pH readings on both the tank and the remaining water in the bucket. Before introducing the fish to the tank water, you need to acclimate them gradually to the existing conditions in the tank. This will entail bringing the bucket water temperature to within 3 degrees of the tank water. If the pH readings also differ, it will be necessary to bring the pH of the bucket water closer to the tank water by at least half of the difference in readings. You accomplish the temperature or pH changes by adding 2 to 3 cups of tank water to the bucket water every 15 minutes until your temperature and pH objectives are reached. Then net the fish out of the bucket and release them into the tank. Dispose of the bucket water, and if necessary bring the tank up to the desired water level by the addition of fresh, chlorine-free water which is first brought to within 3 degrees of the tank water temperature.

So when you are moving fish around from water to water "care" is the watchword. During these transitions the key is to be sure that, throughout the process, your fishes are exposed to "friendly" waters.

Chapter 6

GOIN' FISHIN'

```
Setting up the tank
```

"One commits oneself, and *then* one sees!" Thus states an old proverb. So that moment is at hand. I deliberately waited until Chapter 6 to address tank set up so you would understand how an aquarium functions and what keeps fish alive *before* you invest in live fishes. I want even the *first* fishes you buy to live, too.

This chapter tells you how to set up a standard sized (5 1/2 gallons or larger) aquarium. Mini-tanks, the very small tanks, are the subject of Chapter 9.

There are a few basics to remember when setting up a tank:

#1.   Only after the tank is fully prepared and "aged" do you purchase the live occupants. The filled tank - without fish - should sit for 24 hours to allow any volatile chemicals in the water to escape.

#2.   Do not allow soaps or glass cleaners to touch the inside of a tank. In this connection, be careful not to use soap when washing your hands if you will be handling your fish or putting your hands in the fishes' water.

#3.   Make sure that the tank is placed on an absolutely level surface with all edges supported equally. Tanks are heavy and require sturdy support. Water weighs 8.3 lbs per gallon; so, in a 10 gallon aquarium the water alone weighs 83 lbs. (The weight of the tank, gravel, etc. must also be considered.)

#4.   NEVER pick up a tank containing any significant weight in the form of water, gravel or decorations - or you risk the bursting of seals, glass breakage, and personal injury.

#5.   Be alert, cautious and aware that setting up and moving aquariums can be dangerous; broken glass is probably the greatest hazard.

Here, in step-by-step fashion, is how I suggest that you set-up a tank:

Step #1:
If the tank glass already shows hard water lines from mineral deposits, remove them using hot water and a new single edge razor blade. Be careful not to cut the sealing compounds which join the glass plates. If the tank is acrylic, a razor blade will mar it. For acrylic tanks a "plastic/acrylic safe" algae removing pad available at the pet shop is the best solution.

Step #2:
Using a colander, rinse the gravel in hot water until you are satisfied that it is really clean. If you do not have a colander, rinse 5 lbs. at a time in a 5 gallon bucket.

Step #3:
If you are putting a background picture decoration on the outside of the back glass panel, make certain that the glass is first thoroughly clean. To prevent the future possibility of water getting between the scenery and the glass, run a piece of duct tape or electrical tape the length of the tank along the top of the back panel and a piece of tape or electrical tape vertically down each side of the back panel.

Step #4:
If you are installing an undergravel or sponge filter, now is the time to put the filter into the tank. If you have both a gravel and a sponge filter, place the sponge filter on top of the support plate either on top of the gravel or with the gravel covering the sponge.

In an **undergravel** set-up, place the uplift tubes toward the rear of the tank. If there are an uneven number of uplift tubes, set the air valves to supply equal total amounts of air to the uplift tubes on the right and left sides of the tank - irrespective of which side has the extra uplift tube.

Position the discharge nozzles as shown below.

UNDERGRAVEL FILTER FLOW PATTERNS
(Looking Down on Tank)

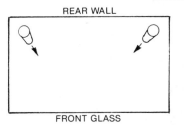

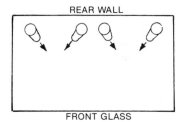

EVEN NUMBER OF UPLIFT TUBES
(Normal Flow)

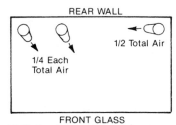

UNEVEN NUMBER OF UPLIFT TUBES
(Circular Flow)

Some **sponge** filter systems are designed to let you control the direction of discharge; some are not. For those permitting directional control, position the filter in a rear corner of the tank and point the discharge nozzle as shown below. (The flow objective might be likened to a 4-cushion billiard shot.)

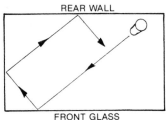

FRONT GLASS
SPONGE FILTER FLOW PATTERN
(Looking Down on Tank)

If you are using an **outside** filter, do not install it at this time. Outside filters can be installed after the tank is filled.

Step #5:

Now put the rinsed gravel into the tank. The gravel should be slightly deeper at the rear of the tank and slope gently toward the front. Also pile gravel slightly higher around the base of any uplift tubes in the tank.

Step #6:

Using an inexpensive test kit (available in pet shops), test your water source for chlorine. If it contains chlorine, before putting any in the tank dechlorinate it using inexpensive chemicals available at your pet shop.

Step #7:

Carefully fill 3/4 of the tank with water making sure that the tank is completely stable and its position does not shift in response to the increasing weight of the water. Decide in advance how you will deal with the problem of incoming water disrupting your carefully placed gravel - either break the flow of the incoming pour, or repair gravel damage afterwards. (If you happen to have three hands, this is a good place to use them.)

Step #8:

Now is the time to put decorations and plants in - before topping off. When accomplished, fill to rim of the tank so the top surface of the water is not visible from the front when the hood is in place.

Step #9:

Turn on the filtering equipment and allow the tank to "age" without fish for 24 hours. This gives the water an opportunity to expel air released from the gravel, for volatile gases to escape, and for the tank filtration equipment to set up an even circulation pattern.

Step #10:

Before going to the store to buy fish, consult Chapter 1 regarding how many fish to start with and the proper way to handle tank start-up. During the next few weeks you will be experiencing the nitrification cycle. Read again carefully in Chapter 1 about this critical period of cycling to stability.

Step #11:

Decide which fish you want to buy and go to the fish store to select your fish. You will find Chapter 10 useful in making this decision.

Step #12:

Go back to Chapter 5 and study the acclimation procedures suggested for introducing your fish to the aquarium. Proceed to introduce your new fish to the aquarium.

Step Down:

This is what I'll call the last step: If all goes well, you can now rest - with watchful eye on the cycling tank. Meanwhile, enjoy your very own beautiful tropical fish swimming in your very own aquatic wonderland.

And, by the way - I have not discussed the many options and choices available in equipment, plants and decorations. There will be these and other matters you will need to discuss with your pet store operator before setting up your aquarium. You should consult a pet store operator for help with auxiliary equipment such as heater, thermostat, hood, etc. and for help with plant selections if you so desire. If your pet shop salesperson is experienced and capable and willing, you will have a partner. Pick your fishpersons carefully; find someone whose opinion you respect and whom you like and trust.

Tell 'em Sarah sent you.

Chapter 7

TROUBLED WATERS

Health problems

Problem detection

Problem solving

Something fishy's going on! What appropriate words to describe that nagging sense that all is not well in your tank!

When health problems occur in your fish population, often your first indication will be an awareness of fish behaving in an unusual or uncharacteristic manner. Among the common signs of health problems are listless behavior, failure to feed, and unusually rapid movement of the gills. You may notice a fish repeatedly rubbing its body against decorations or equipment. A fish's color may become faded. The fins of a fish may appear ragged or may seem pinned to its body, immobile and not extended in the normal manner. A sick fish may tend to remain in one place instead of swimming about and may also wiggle its body back and forth and contort as if in pain. Erratic or uncharacteristic behavior should always be cause for concern. It almost inevitably signals distress caused by ill health.

Aquarium fish are vulnerable to health problems which fall into four major categories - **poisoning** by ammonia or sulphites, **injury** evidenced by wounds or burns, **disease** usually in the form of fungal or parasitic infection, and **stress**. Lets look at that last one first, the catch-all "stress".

Stress:

Aquarists often refer to ill fish as "stressed". Just as stress in humans has many causes so, too, does fish stress. And the effect of stress on fish is also similar to the effect of stress on humans. Fish can come under stress because they feel threatened by either their tank mates or by their environment, or because they are suffering from illness or injury. Stress also makes them vulnerable to illness and injury, so it can be either a cause, or an effect, or both at once.

Just as humans do, "stressed" fish often exhibit erratic behavior while suffering deteriorating health.

It is not always easy to determine the causes of stress. A physical examination may show visible signs of injury, disease, or infection. Poisoning and internal infection may not be revealed by external inspection. Any of these may result in erratic or "stressed" behavior. One of the most prevalent causes of stress, however, is the population mix in the tank. Some species of fish must be with their own kind to prosper. Others cannot co-exist well with their own kind or with some other species. Sometimes big fish threaten smaller fish. It may be that the tank arrangements do not provide the cover from predators that a certain species requires. Some kinds of fish require places to hide - "territories" provided by arrangement of tank decorations to form "caves" or fenced-off areas. Temperature fluctuations, too much or too little light, proper food supply - all can bring on stress.

Poisoning:

Ammonia or nitrite poisoning come about because the biological filter system is not providing adequate bacteria to remove these poisoning agents. This indicates that there are too many fish, or that filtering capacity is inadequate, or that filters are not operating properly, or that too much food is being put into the water.

Injury:

Injuries can be in the form of wounds, usually inflicted by other fish (termed "aggression"), or as burns caused by excessive ammonia or nitrite in the water.

Disease:

Fungal infections usually result in easily seen cotton- like or slimy growths on the fish. Not infrequently the fungal infection starts as a secondary effect of an injury. **Parasitic infections** usually cause visible malformations. The most frequently encountered parasitic infection found in tropical and coldwater fish is Ichthyophthrius Multifilis, called **Ich**, and pronounced "ick". Evidence of Ich are little protrusions on the body or fins about the size of a pinhead and resembling grains of salt. There may be only a few or there may be many. In cases of fish deaths, if before death they can be seen to be breathing heavily you should suspect external parasites such as **flukes** (which are microscopic in size). Another possible indication of flukes is, if prior to death, fish are observed diving at objects in the tank to rub their bodies against something solid (called "**scratching**").

What to look for / what to do:

I can't over-emphasize the importance of water chemistry; *keep the water free of ammonia and nitrites*. These chemicals are the direct cause of poisoning and burns; moreover, when other health problems are experienced - such as wounds, infection or stress, these chemicals both aggravate the condition and make cure more difficult or impossible. After making sure that tank temperatures and temperature fluctuation are under control, *getting water test readings for ammonia, nitrite and pH to the proper levels, and getting the biological filtering mechanism to perform effectively should be your most immediate concern* in treating any and all health problems - even when aggression is the obvious cause. When tests show that ammonia and nitrite are present in harmful quantities, the corrective procedure varies. It depends upon the nature and the severity of the existing condition. In Chapter 8 I have spelled out a step- by-step explanation of what to do under varying circumstances to correct improper water conditions. Chapter 8 is devoted entirely to the various ways to "fix the water".

One more time: **when health problems of any kind occur, immediately test the ammonia, nitrite and pH levels. If they are not right, fix them. Refer to Chapter 8**. Now lets look at *what else* to do.

Poisoning:

If you have "fixed" the water you've stopped the ammonia and nitrite poisoning. Nothing else is necessary.

Disease:

Some of the visible signs of fungal infections and parasitic infections were described above. When detected or suspected, first look to curing any water conditions problems which exist. In my experience 9 out of 10 fungal infections are either caused by, or aggravated by, improper water conditions. A good pet shop will recommend and supply antibiotics for fungal infections and other medications for parasitic infections. Before treating the water with medication, get the water clear and the test readings acceptable. Be aware that antibiotic medications can affect the "good" bacteria colonies adversely so while treating the water take frequent test readings. If test readings deteriorate, stop medication and correct the water conditions before resuming. Parasitic medications - other than those containing formalin or methylene blue - do not harm the bacteria and therefore also serve well as a preventative measure whenever parasites are suspected. If your tank contains any of the kind of fish which are inherently less immune than most (so-called "scaleless" fish in the trade), such as catfish and tetras, take special care in regulating medication and consult a pet shop before beginning treatment. In the cases of parasitic infections, before resorting to medication try increasing tank temperature to about 82 degrees F. for 24 hours. Afterwards if parasites persist, medication treatment should begin.

Injury and Stress:

If the injury appears to be a **burn** on the fish's slime coat (ie: "skin") or if the slime coat is actually ulcerated, the cause is undoubtedly ammonia or nitrite in the water. Your water tests will confirm this. The obvious solution is to bring the water test readings into line. Refer to Chapter 8 for guidance.

Wounds are almost always caused by other fish, and some sort of change in the population or change in the environment is required. Lets take up the subject of wounds and **stress** together.

A fish may exhibit signs of stress for any of the reasons mentioned earlier in this chapter. Faded color often signals a stress victim. Behavioral signs such as hiding in the decorations or corners of the tank can be signs of victimization. If you see a fish behaving in a manner which suggests stress, first look for the visible signs of burns, or of fungal or parasitic infection. Then make sure the water tests for ammonia, nitrites and pH are satisfactory. Satisfy yourself that tank temperatures are not excessive and do not fluctuate more than 4 degrees F in a short period of time. Next check up on your fish's peculiarities in the *Fishbuyer's Fishfinder* (Chapter 10) to determine whether your tank provides the individual living and environmental conditions this particular fish requires. These steps will probably reveal the likely cause of the stress. If the probable cause is still not identified, then whether or not you see actual wounds such as frayed fins and tails, you should still conclude that some of your tank tenants are incompatible and that the fish mix needs changing. More close observation and a little more research in Chapter 10 should produce guidance. When aggression is occurring, the perpetrator will often be a fish that is almost never found in hiding places, is the first to eat at feeding time, and shows the brightest body coloration.

If the problem is incompatibility or aggression and it becomes necessary to change the fish population, an obvious choice is to get rid of the aggressor. Sometimes, however, you might elect the opposite choice and replace the peaceful fish with aggressive ones more capable of defense. If mild cases of aggression are occurring but not causing deaths, sometimes adding or changing decorations to better define or expand territories will lessen the attacks.

Coping with failure:

No one enjoys seeing their fishes expire; but, inevitably there will be times when you have to cope with a dead fish or two. It will be obvious to some, but perhaps not to all, that the simplest, quickest and least traumatic way to deal with the problem is to net out the dead fish and dispatch it to the toilet forthwith.

More fixing to come:

This chapter has been about identifying and coping with common problems. Regardless of the nature of the problem, I have emphasized the need to bring and keep in line ammonia, nitrite and pH test readings. The next chapter explains in detail how to do just that - how to "cure bad water".

Chapter 8

WRING OUT THE OLD

Replacing "bad" water

Curing Water Chemistry

This important chapter will tell you how to go about curing chemically sick water. I'll admit that this is probably not anyone's idea of a fun chapter. I'll even suggest that you just skim it for now. If you do a reasonably careful job of operating your aquarium, you should not need these procedures often - if at all. But, if and when you need them, you know where they are.

How do you regain control of water chemistry that is out of control? Obviously one logical and appropriate corrective action is gradual replacement of a portion of the existing "bad" tank water with "new" water that is free of the problems. Another frequently appropriate corrective action is simply to reduce the amount of food put in the water. Even though your biological filter system has adequate size and capacity for your fish population when fed properly, it still may prove ineffective if you are overfeeding - putting more food in the tank than the fish will eat quickly. Food reduction and water changes are the chief corrective measures to take, but when to do which and how much to do depends upon exactly what is wrong and how bad it is.

In any change of tank water, *gradual* replacement is the goal. This chapter, however, frequently recommends a change of much more of the tank water than the 1/4 to 1/3 tank amounts suggested earlier for routine water changes in a healthy tank. Critical conditions sometimes call for drastic actions.

You should become familiar with the pH of your tap water so you can predict the pH effect of adding untreated tap water. Obviously, you don't want to add acid tap water to an already acid tank; so, if the tap water is acidic, treat it with **sodium bicarbonate** (buffering up) before adding any of it to the tank. Also, you should know whether your tap water contains chlorine which must be removed before your use in the aquarium.

CAUTION: During the changes of tank water and reductions in feeding suggested in this chapter, it is desirable to avoid disturbing the filter media to protect the bacteria colonies growing there. If, however, filters become clogged, they must be unclogged. Do so - but, as carefully as possible.

The appropriate corrective steps differ depending upon whether the problems are occurring in alkaline or slightly acid waters (pH of 6.8 or higher) or in highly acid waters (pH below 6.8). So before deciding what corrective procedures to follow, determine the pH of the tank water. Let's discuss acid water first.

Problem Water Under HIGHLY ACID CONDITIONS: (pH lower than 6.8) Slightly acid waters in the pH range of 6.8 to 7.0 are included below with "Problem Water Under Alkaline Conditions"

We know that an acid condition means that the bacteria which we count upon for eliminating ammonia and nitrites will not be performing efficiently. So even if levels of ammonia or nitrite are not yet high, we should bring the pH up to at least 6.9. Bring it up higher if it appears likely that in the near future the tank may contain additional detritus (debris), or wood, or plants - all of which act to lower pH.

The water changes recommended below for acid tanks will be effective only if the replacement water is alkaline. Prior to adding tap water, test it's acidity. If necessary, add sodium bicarbonate to the tap water to bring its pH up to an alkaline range of 7.0 to 7.6.

1. If there is no **ammonia** *or* **nitrite** present, simply bring the pH up to 6.9 or higher by changing 1/3 to 1/2 of the tank water every 2 or 3 days until pH is satisfactory. If the water is very acidic - a pH of 6.6 or lower - make 1/2 tank changes on a daily basis until pH climbs to at least 7.0. When adding the new water, do so gradually over a 30 minute period so as to lessen the shock to the fishes from an abrupt pH change.

2. If **ammonia** is not present but **nitrite** is above 1 mg/liter, start water changes of 1/3 to 1/2 tank every other day to bring the pH up. As the water becomes less acid, the nitrobacter bacteria will become more efficient converters of nitrite to nitrate. The nitrite should dissipate at least within two weeks and perhaps as rapidly as a few days. If this fails to occur, it suggests either that you are overfeeding the fish

or that too many fish are in the tank for the capacity of the bacteriological (biological) filter. (Although not very likely, it is possible that in areas with acid local waters, a tank with these symptoms might only be cycling.) If the pH is as low as 6.6 or lower, make 1/2 tank changes daily. When adding the new water, do so gradually over a 30 minute period so as to lessen the shock to the fishes from an abrupt pH change.

3. If **ammonia** is above 1 ppm but **nitrite** is not present, consider whether the biological filtration provided is adequate for the fish population involved. If filtration capacity is believed adequate, then the nitrosomonas bacteria are not performing efficiently because of acid water, and you must raise the pH so they can do their job.

If the water **acidity is no lower than** a pH of **6.6** - *or* if the **ammonia is no higher than 2 ppm** (parts per million), make 1/2 to 3/4 tank changes on a daily basis until the ammonia is removed and the pH satisfactory.

If **acidity is lower than 6.6**, *or* if **ammonia is greater than 2 ppm**, stop all feeding and make 3/4 tank changes daily until the pH climbs to 6.6 and the ammonia falls to 2 ppm. At that point resume feeding and reduce water changes to 1/2 to 3/4 tank.

When adding the new water, do so gradually over a 30 minute period so as to lessen the shock to the fishes from an abrupt pH change.

NOTE: There is a serious difficulty under conditions of high ammonia in a highly acid tank. In such an environment ammonia is technically *ammonium* - which is less toxic to the fish than ammonia. As we bring the pH up past 6.8 (which we must do to prevent deterioration into situation #4, below), the ammonium changes into the more toxic ammonia. This is a dilemma because it causes the fish to undergo extreme stress and often proves fatal. If alternative holding facilities (established tanks) are available, the risk of fish loss can be reduced by moving the fish to these facilities. Although placing fish abruptly into this new environment will also be very stressful for the fish and may well result in some losses, I believe that this alternative is less stressful than subjecting them to the drastic water changes required. If placed in an alternative facility, they should remain there until the original tank pH is above 6.8 and the ammonia below 1 ppm. (See Chapter 5 for precautions.)

4. If **ammonia** is 3 ppm or above and **nitrite** is 4-5 mg/liter, the situation is very serious.

If, the **acidity measures no lower than 6.6, and** the **ammonia concentration is lower than 2 ppm,** *and* the **nitrite concentration is lower than 3 mg/liter** - start water changes of 1/2 to 3/4 tank daily until the pH is satisfactory and both ammonia and nitrite are under control. When adding the new water, do so gradually over a 30 minute period so as to lessen the shock to the fishes from an abrupt pH change.

If **ammonia** *or* **nitrite are at levels greater than these,** correction would require water and feeding changes so drastic that the fish would not be likely to survive. On the other hand, unless something is done quickly the fish will die anyway from the poisons in the water. **If an alternative holding facility** with "good" water is available, move the fish to it, while correcting the chemistry of the "bad" water with water changes of 1/2 tank each day. (See the note in paragraph 3, above, for a discussion of the relative risks involved.) Do not return the fish to the tank until the pH is above 6.8, ammonia is below 2 ppm, and nitrite is below .25 mg/liter. **If no alternative holding facility** is available, the only remedy available is to place the fish in temporary containers still in the "bad" water, tear the tank down completely, and start up again with new water. It is a good idea to drop an airstone into the temporary container and aerate the "bad" water. Establish new bacteria colonies by again proceeding through the nitrification cycle as described in Chapter 5. Under such circumstances the risk of fish loss will be even greater but unavoidable.

Consider again whether the filter system is adequate.

If an undergravel tank is to be torn down completely, it is still possible to preserve at least a small portion of the existing bacteria to seed the new gravel bed. This is accomplished by removing about 1/20th of the gravel, rinsing it free of debris with unchlorinated room temperature water, and then keeping it dampened with unchlorinated room temperature water. When the aquarium is set-up again, use this gravel to place on top of the new gravel bed to "re-seed" the bed with bacteria.

**Problem Water Under ALKALINE *or* SLIGHTLY ACID CONDI-
TIONS:** (pH of 6.8 or higher)

1. If **ammonia** and **nitrite** levels are satisfactory, you have been doing your water chemistry job well. Enjoy a moment of self congratulation.

2. If **ammonia** is not present, but **nitrite** levels are above .1 mg/liter, the tank is probably in the last 1 or 2 weeks of the process of cycling toward stability (see Chapter 1). Give it a chance to complete the cycle; just feed the fish lightly and continue to monitor. If nitrite readings are extremely high, above 10 mg/liter, (the water will also be highly alkaline) make 1/3 to 1/2 changes of the tank water until the nitrite appears under control.

3. If **ammonia** is higher than 1 ppm but no **nitrite** is indicated, it is likely that the tank is in the early stages of the nitrifica-tion cycle and that the nitrite will peak and gradually dissipate as the nitrobacter bacteria colony multiplies to meet its growing food supply. Be aware that this might not be what is happening and monitor closely to guard against nitrite levels building and conditions becoming those in 4, below. If the ammonia level is higher than 3 ppm, make 1/3 to 1/2 tank water changes daily until the ammonia drops to 3 ppm.

4. If **ammonia** is above 1 ppm and **nitrite** is above .1 mg/liter, consider the possibility that the biological filtration provided may not be adequate for the fish population involved. If you believe filtration is adequate, stop feeding entirely and start 3/4 tank changes of water once a day until the ammonia is gone and readings have returned to condition 2, above. At this point feed every other day until nitrite also dissipates.

Leaving troubles behind:

The last two chapters have been devoted to procedures necessary to coping with the health problems which may arise in your fish population. When health problems do arise, it serves no purpose to ignore them. Fast remedial action is the wise course. In the case of the more serious and contagious problems, ignoring these for even a short time can put your entire fish community in jeopardy.

Chapter 9

LOWER SCALES

> The Mini-tank

"Look, Mommy, I won a goldfish!" Oh, oh! That just could be the start of your mini-tank experience.

The youngest of the brood returns home from the local community fair with a small plastic bag, filled with water and one, not-too-happy goldfish. What to do! You think you have options; but you really haven't. You can either find a way to keep this fish alive - or . . . you can live through postmortem days filled with heartrending sobbing and "WhyDidGoldyDie"s before you decide to buy goldfish number two. Either way, the problem is the same. You have at least one goldfish; and, now you want to keep it alive.

You could, if you wish, actually try a goldfish bowl - without filtration; but be prepared to change all the water and clean the bowl about every three days. Each time the new water must be brought to the temperature of the old, the fish must be acclimated gradually to the new waters; and, various other cautions apply. I won't go into a detailed discussion of goldfish bowls. I'll assume that you are at least going to opt for what we call a mini-tank.

When I talk about mini-tanks, I'm referring to any small, filtered, plastic tank holding less than 5 gallons of water. Mini-tanks are usually sold as kits including a small under-gravel filter and a 15 watt incandescent light. Typically these mini-tanks are the product of a novelty manufacturer not regularly engaged in producing larger aquariums. The height of these small volume tanks is often about the same as the height of a 10 gallon tank, but since the capacity is less, all the other dimensions are also less. A common type of mini-tank is a hexagonal-sided, tower-like structure which is deeper than it is wide. This peculiar shape causes the mini-tank to have a small water surface area in proportion to volume. The small surface area has less capacity to entrap air, and therefore limits the size of the fish population. There is also only sufficient bottom area for a gravel bed which will be small in proportion to the volume of water in the tank. With only a small gravel bed and limited aeration of the water, it is difficult to establish bacteria colonies, and difficult to supply adequate oxygen to the fish and to the bacteria colonies.

Finally, the mini-tanks typically do not come with a heater or thermostat control. The incandescent bulb which may come with the kit burns very hot and is not a satisfactory heat source. Installing a heat source that can be regulated will probably be necessary to keep temperature fluctuations from exceeding 4 degrees - about the most that most tropical fish can be certain to withstand. Fish of the goldfish and carp families, although prolific producers of ammonia, have perhaps the best chance of surviving temperature changes greater than 4 degrees.

While I will tell you how to operate a mini-tank - more- or-less successfully - you should understand that it is not exactly easy. It takes a certain amount of dedication and determination to keep fish alive in one of these inexpensive aquariums (which are sometimes called "Desktop" tanks). But, let's say that you have the "right stuff"; here's how I suggest that you approach the challenge.

First, in a new tank, install the under-gravel filter with 3-4 lbs. of fine grade gravel. Before putting the gravel on top of the support plate, thoroughly rinse and clean the gravel in hot water. The gravel on the support plate should be about 2 1/2 to 3 inches deep. 3 to 4 lbs. should provide that depth. Fill the tank with water (which has first been dechlorinated if your water supply contains chlorine), start the air pump and allow the filter system to operate for at least 24 hours before putting fish in it. By that time the temperature and flow patterns in the tank will have reached a consistent and stable condition. (Incidentally, when little WhyDidGoldyDie came home with #1 fish, you had no 24 hours to spend on tank start up. Goldy had to take on more risk than I prefer or recommend; but, alas, in fish life, too, sometimes expedient measures must do.)

After the tank has reached a stable operating condition (24 hours), introduce the fish to the mini-tank. Acclimate in the same manner as described in Chapter 5. With the fish in a plastic bag containing 1/2 to 1 cup of the water to which it is already accustomed (and containing about two thirds air), float the bag on the tank water surface for 10 to 15 minutes. Then add a cup of aquarium water to the bag; float again for 10 to 15 minutes and release into the tank.

Start to feed the fish based upon 1 flake of food per 1 1/2 fish inches (doesn't include tails) either once a day, or preferably, once every other day. Rather than 1/4 to 1/3 tank water changes, plan to do about 1/2 tank water changes (in the manner described in CHAPTER 5) once or twice a week and watch for the tank to complete the nitrification cycle described in Chapter 1. In a mini-tank expect the nitrification cycle to require more time - perhaps 6 to 8 weeks, rather than 4 to 6.

Upon completion of the nitrification cycle, you should perform the first gravel rinse, and you may now add another feeding time and increase the total amount of food - but certainly no more than double what you had been providing.

If this happens to be your first aquarium and you do not have testing equipment to determine the status of the nitrification cycle, 8 to 10 weeks should be a sufficient wait before the initial gravel rinse and 12 weeks before increasing feedings.

After the first gravel rinse, repeat the procedure every 2 to 3 months, and the half tank water changes every 3 to 4 weeks. Whenever you remove fish or change the make-up of aquarium water with partial water changes, be sure to use the acclimation procedures described in Chapter 5 when reintroducing fish to the tank.

The best time to rinse gravel is during a water change. Remove the gravel carefully and rinse only about half in hot water. Allow the rest of the gravel to remain unrinsed; but, keep it damp with used water from the aquarium in order to preserve a portion of the established colony of bacteria. Then place the cleaned gravel back on the support plate and the unrinsed gravel on top of the cleaned gravel to "re-seed" the bacterial population.

In a mini-tank it is not unusual to find that algae growth becomes a problem. If it does, I suggest periodic treatment with a chemical algicide in dosages recommended by your pet shop. I suggest also that you limit lighting of the tank to no more than 12 hours a day.

Number and kinds of fish:

If the fish you choose are larger than 1 inch in length (without including length of tail), there should be no more than 2 fish during the period of the start-up nitrification cycle. If the fish are only 1/2 to 1 inch in length, you can probably have a third fish in the tank if you wish.

As I mentioned before, the mini-tank is a poor home for tropical fish but somewhat better for goldfish or cold water fishes. If, understanding this, you would still like to try your hand at some tropicals, I have had fair success with members of the Barb family - which are fishes with considerable endurance and resistance to temperature variations. White Cloud Mountain Fish and common Guppies are other species which offer some hope of survival. (See Chapter 10 for more detailed descriptions of these species.)

So, as we told you in the introduction, once again we find that smaller is harder - but it isn't all *that* hard.

Chapter 10

THE FISHBUYER'S FISHFINDER

---

100 fish characterizations

Compatibility guide

Suggested fish groups

280 common name identifier

This chapter is about fish compatibility. It's about selecting the right fish for your aquarium. It's about realizing the most enjoyment, and it's about suffering the fewest hassles. It's about how individual fish can be expected to behave - in a small aquarium. This chapter will describe the in-tank characteristics of many different fish. It will guide you to beauty, action and interest in your aquarium. It will, also, help keep you from wasting money by buying fish that have little chance of surviving together. This chapter, we hope, will keep your hobby from "eating you alive".

The *Fishbuyer's Fishfinder* is a reference made up of this section and three additional sections identified as follows:

FINDER ONE -   a numbered list describing **100** fish in detail.

FINDER TWO -   a list of **280** fish names, keyed to the numbers in FINDER ONE.

FINDER THREE -   eleven fish groupings I have found to feature . . beauty . . interest . . excitement . . fascination. The fish in each group are identified by their FINDER ONE numbers.

SOME FEATURES OF THE FINDERS:
In FINDER ONE, among other things, I have identified those

fish that seem to require other members of their breed as companions in order to flourish. These are termed either "*pair*" fish or "*school*" fish - suggesting their preferences for being with at least one additional member of their own kind in the case of pair fish, or at least two additional members in the case of school fish. While such fish can survive as one of a kind, they suffer less stress and are therefore more frequently visible and have better color, if their gregarious preferences are honored. (You have seen people grow pale when ill? Well, many fish show significant color loss when stressed.)

Those fish not marked "pair" or "school" are shown as "*single*" fish. The "single" label covers two different categories: 1) fish independent enough to do well *with or without* other members of their species present, and 2) fish which simply do not get along with others of their own kind - either because of their territorial nature, or because they compete with each other for food supply (as in the case of algae-eaters). FINDER ONE individual fish descriptions tell which category applies.

FINDER ONE also differentiates "*egg-layers*" from "*live-bearers*". Egg-layers lay eggs which are fertilized and the embryo brought to anatomical maturity outside the fish's body. Live-bearers give birth to live fry which are already anatomically developed.

SOME OBSERVATIONS ABOUT COMPATIBILITY:

You will want to buy for your aquarium fish which are likely to survive and prosper in each other's company and not be hostile or stressful to each other. You want them to enhance visually your aquarium and to complement each other. If you'll pardon the pun, this chapter is dedicated to just that - "fishing for complements".

Compatibility depends upon many factors. One is size in relation to other tank members. A fish that can fit into the mouth of a larger neighbor is always in some danger of ending up there. For those species that have strong territorial instinct, another factor is the availability of a defined, identifiable area of the tank which can be claimed as their own. Places to hide are important to some fish. Eating habits can conflict. Certain kinds of fish tend to inhabit a tank at different depths. Some fish can be identified as "surface-swimming", "bottom-swimming" or "middle-swimming", and an attractive, balanced tank will probably contain all three. Species that might not tolerate each other at the same depth can nevertheless often reside peacefully in a tank where they seldom meet because of their differing swimming preferences.

You know the expression, "People are funny!"? Well, fish are funny, too. At least they often act "funny". No one can be absolutely sure that one day old Aunt Finny will not turn on old Uncle Gilly and put him away for good. Fish can be unpredictable and, people-like, seem to have individual personalities. So conviction about fish compatibility builds from personal experience and successful experimentation. My recommendations are those that I personally have found workable. Some of my selections do not agree with others I have read elsewhere. Many I have read fail to mention aggressive and destructive behavior that I have found quite predictable. I think that some of the selections in print stem from experience with "big" aquariums. Often fish varieties that can tolerate each other in a large tank do not have the room to stay out of each other's way in a smaller tank. What works in a 55 gallon tank just may not work in a 10 or 20 gallon tank.

Even if it were possible for me to have detailed knowledge of your aquarium and your fish community, I would still be making judgment calls when I suggest additional fish to enhance your enjoyment. In this chapter I attempt to offer conservative and cautious guidance about who will swim with whom - in swimmingly fashion. The choices are those that I have personally found workable with predictable consistency. I hope they work for you as they have for me.

BETTER FISHING TIPS:

Tip #1: When you go to the store to select new fish (or - forgive the term - *replacement* fish), take this book with you. If you use these pages in the fish store, you just may not have to go there quite so often.

Tip #2: At the end of this book you will find a form for keeping track of your tank population. Keep it up to date. If kept properly it will prove valuable when you select additional fish for your aquariums. Take it with you to the fish store to use in discussions with your pet shop operator. Many fish have more than one name; sometimes names are similar and confusing. For that reason I suggest that whenever you buy new fish, ask the pet shop operator personally to write the names in your record so that at future discussion and recommendation times the pet shop operator can be confidently knowledgeable about the make-up of your existing population. The pet shop operator's knowledge will be of much more value about everything from medicines and filters to fish selections *if* the store person truly *knows* what's in *your* tank.

THE FISHBUYER'S FISHFINDER

- FINDER ONE -

COMMONLY AVAILABLE FRESH WATER TROPICAL FISH

1.   **Algae Eater, Chinese** ("Al-Gee")   *Gyrinocheilus aymonieri*

All-depths swimmer; single fish; egg-layer; not bred in captivity

Although a very good algae eater when young, as it ages it's dietary preferences change and it may become aggressive toward other fish. Aggression may also result from inadequate supply of algae. (This fish should not be acquired until algae is evident in the tank.) This fish and any listed here as "compatible" with it, may consume any fish small enough to fit in its mouth or any which is not fast enough to escape it. When small and supplied with ample algae this fish will do well with almost any fish of its size; however, when it gets older it is only compatible with fish it cannot catch - such as these:

Compatible fish: #10; and no more than one of either #73, #75 or #76; and school fish #7, #8, #32, #34, #67; and pair fish #15, #23, #25, #39, #43, #46, #54, #58, #71, #72, #77

2.   **Angelfish** - entire group   *Pterophllum scalare*

Middle-to-surface swimmer; pair fish; egg-layer; commonly bred in captivity

These fish have an unpredictable compatibility.   They are peaceful fish when small but grow extremely rapidly, and as they grow become increasingly aggressive; so yesterday's playmate can become tomorrow's dinner. When young they will get along with any fish that does not fit in their mouth. When older they become more aggressive and should be kept with faster more durable fish such as the following:

Compatible fish: #19, #66; and no more than one of either #73, #75 or #76; and school fish #33, #69, #97; and school fish #81, #87, #89,

#93, #58 as long as they are not much smaller than the Angelfish; and pair fish #12, #56, #59, #72

3. **Arowana** ("Air-Roe-Wah-Nah")   *Osteoglossum bicirrhosum*

Surface-swimmer; single fish; mouth breeder; not bred in captivity

This is an ancient, pre-historic fish that retains many primitive characteristics. Very young specimens are often shipped with a visible yoke-sac present which, for a period, continues to supply nourishment. This fish is a notorious jumper and will leave a tank which is not very tightly covered. It is docile when young but grows rapidly and will devour anything which will fit in its out-sized mouth. The enormous mouth drops open in a fashion reminiscent of World War II landing ships. This fish can grow up to six feet in length. The common Arowana is a pearly iridescent fish with a full body fin under the body.

Compatible fish: Because of its rapid growth, the mix of fishes with which it can co-exist also changes rapidly. This fish will get along with any non-aggressive fish which is also too large to be eaten by the Arowana.

4. **Barb, Cherry**   *Capoeta titteya*

Bottom swimmer; school fish; egg-layer; commonly bred in captivity

These fish are small-mouthed, relatively peaceful members of the Barb family. They do not grow as large as most other Barbs. When in breeding color they are often a brilliant red; the females are somewhat paler in color than the males. Although not bottom feeders as such, they do frequently feed along the bottom and sometimes dine on algae. As true with other Barbs, they have a fair tolerance for temperature fluctuation.

Compatible fish: #19, #66; and school fish #5, #13, #34, #68, #80, #90, #98, and pair fish #12, #38, #56, #57, #59, #61, #65, #50, #78, #99

5. **Barb, Gold**   *Puntius sachsi*

Middle swimmer; school fish; egg-layer; commonly bred in
captivity

These fish are relatively peaceful members of the Barb family.
Compared to most other members of the Barb family they
remain small. These are yellow-golden fish with a checkerboard
stripe running from the eye to the tail.
They get along with any other Barbs which are not large enough
to eat them. As true with other Barbs, they have a fair tolerance for temperature fluctuation.

Compatible fish: #19, #66; and school fish #4, #13, #34;
                     #68, #80, #90, #98, and pair fish #12,
                     #38, #56, #57, #59 #61, #65, #50, #78,
                     #99

6. **Barb, Rosy**   *Puntius conchonius*

Bottom-to-middle swimmer; school fish; egg-layer; commonly
bred in captivity

This is a relatively peaceful and a mid-sized member of the
Barb family. As with other members of the Barb family, the
more there are of their own species, the less aggressive they are.
They get along well with all other Barbs which are not large
enough to eat them. One hybrid of the species has exceptionally
long, fluid, graceful fins. The females of this species are
considerably duller and almost brown; thus, the name derives
from the males. The brilliant red of the males is most apparent
when in the presence of females. This species is efficient in
cleaning up the hairy ("filamentacious") type of algae.

Compatible fish: #66; and no more than one of either #73,
                     #75 or #76, and school fish #7, #8, #32,
                     #34, #96, #97, #98; and pair fish #12,
                     #39, #43, #44, #45, #46, #47, #56, #63,
                     #58, #60, - as long as none of these pair
                     fish are much larger than the Rosy.

7. **Barb, Tiger**   *Capoeta tetrazona*

Middle swimmer; school fish; egg-layer; bred in captivity

There are many members of this family and they all mix well together. They are a medium-sized group of Barbs and are extremely aggressive for their size. They are hardy fish, somewhat tolerant of temperature fluctuations. These fish are fin-nippers if not kept in schools. Their preference, however, is to chase each other rather than other fish.

Compatible fish: #66; and no more than one of either #73, #75 or #76; and school fish #6, #8, #32, #34; and pair fish #12, #23, #25, #39, #43, #44, #45, #46, #47, #56, #63, #54, #60 - provided that none of these pair fish are larger than the Tiger.

8. **Barb, Tin Foil**   *Barbodes schwanenfeldi*

Middle swimmer; school fish; egg-layer; not bred in captivity in this country

These are called "Tin Foil" because they are silvery in color. The silver bodies, however, frequently are "framed" by fins which are red, black or a variation thereof. These are very fast swimmers. As with other members of the Barb family, the more there are of their own species, the less aggressive they are. They grow to become two to three times larger than any other of the Barb species. They tend to swim in tighter schools than most school fish. When not kept in schools they tend to be markedly more aggressive and "nippy".

Compatible fish: #66; and no more than one of either #73, #75 or #76 and school fish #6, #7, #32, #34; and pair fish #12, #23, #25, #39, #30, #43, #44, #45, #46 #47, #56, #63, #54, #71, #72 - provided that none of these pair fish are larger than the Tin Foil.

9. **Bettas** ("Bay-Tuz" or "Bet-Us")   *Betta splendens*
    entire group

All-depths swimmer; single fish; egg-layer; commonly bred in captivity

There are many members of this family and they vary in color from red, violet, blue, albino, black, and a rare green. This fish is not predictable as a compatible community member; it is best kept alone - one fish to a tank. . or, as is fairly common, a bowl or mini-tank. Although there is an occasional gregarious Betta, the male is extremely territorial and will usually try to kill any other male Betta within its territory - and sometimes females, as well. This fish is only energetic when fighting or displaying for breeding. When prepared to fight, it becomes dramatically altered in appearance. The top fins come up; the bottom fins go down; the tail fin spreads; the gill plates are thrust out; and, in general, it appears to grow immensely - attempting to awe and terrify the opponent. Even seeing its own reflection can trigger this fight response. It is a "picky" eater and prefers krill or brine shrimp.

10. **Botia** ("Bow-Tee-Ah") *(many species)*
    entire family

Bottom swimmer; pair fish; egg-layer; not bred in captivity

There are many different species of Botias. These fish have barely visible, recessed spines on each side of the face which serve both as a weapon and a defensive mechanism. Another fish does not eat a Botia face-first without consequences. They prefer numerous hiding places to dash in and out of. They are capable of making a clearly audible clicking sound. These fish prefer to be in pairs but like to make their own selection of partners. Sometimes trial and error is necessary to establish a compatible pair. Unfortunately this may mean introducing 4 to end up with 2. These fish, and all listed here as "compatible" with them, may eat whatever fish they can fit into their mouths or any which is not fast enough to escape them. These fish will do well with whatever they can't catch.

Compatible fish: #66; and no more than one of either #73, #75 or #76 and school fish #7, #8, #32, #34, #67 and pair fish #15, #23, #25, #39, #42, #30, #43, #45, #46, #47, #63, #60

11. **Butterfly Fish**   *Pantodon buchholzi*

Surface swimmer; pair fish; egg-layer; not easily bred in captivity

These are beautiful, graceful, slow-growing fish. They have a camouflage-like, speckled appearance. Their trap- door mouth is excellently formed for catching insects, and they will remain almost motionless for hours awaiting something to strike the water surface. They are tank jumpers but will be less so if the surface is partially covered with floating plants.

Compatible fish: #16, #19, #37, #66; and school fish #5, #13, #68; and pair fish #12, #36, #56, #57, #58, #59, #74

12. **Catfish, Corydorus** ("Ko-Ree-Dore-Us")   *(many speciesy* entire family

Bottom swimmer; pair fish; egg-layer; commonly bred in captivity

Many varieties of these adaptable and peaceful fish are sold. These are "busy" tank members - endlessly working in pursuit of food scraps in the gravel. They will be more visible if paired and will also do well with more than two members of the species. These fish will get along with almost any other fishes except Cichlids, or aggressive fish, or much larger fish.

13. **Catfish, Debawi** ("Deb-Ow-Wee")   *Eutropiellus debauwie*

Middle-to-bottom swimmer; school fish; egg-layer; not common-ly bred in captivity

These are bright fish with longitudinal white, black and grey stripes running the full body length. They are peaceful, commu-nity fish, and unlike other catfish will not defend themselves against attack. When with their own kind, they are extremely active and busy.

Compatible fish: #37, #66; and school fish #5, #6, #7, #33, #34, #68, #80, #86, #90, #92, #96, #97, #98, #100; and pair fish #12, #38, #50, #55, #58, #62, #99

14. **Catfish, Glass** *Kryptopterus bicirrhis*

All-depths swimmer; school fish; egg-layer; not commonly bred in captivity

These are transparent fish. They are extremely timid and, even when in schools, tend to hide. The schools typically hover in plants in one area of the tank and, because color is visible through their bodies, the schools are often difficult to see. They can be kept only with very timid companions.

Compatible fish: #19, #66; and school fish #13, #49, #53, #64, #79, #84, #85, #88, #91, #94, #100; and pair fish #35, #59, #62

15. **Catfish, Pictus Pimolodella** *Pimelodus pictus*

Bottom swimmer; pair fish; egg-layer; not bred in captivity

These are beautiful, long-whiskered bottom fish (scavengers); they prosper best in groups of at least two. They are hiding fish and need rock caves and places to hide. Also, they tend to be nocturnal. Although peaceful in nature, these fish do tend to be ever-hungry. They have large mouths and will attempt to devour anything the mouth can encompass even if immediate consumption is physically impossible. Accordingly, they can not be trusted with any fish small enough to enter those mouths.

Compatible fish: Any fish too large for their mouth, except African Cichlids, or South American Cichlids significantly larger than the Catfish.

16. **Catfish, Raphael** ("Raf-Ee-Ell") *Platydorus costatus*

Bottom swimmer; single fish; egg-layer; not bred in captivity

This is a bottom fish, or scavenger. It is a hiding fish and needs places to hide. It also tends to be nocturnal. It is a sturdy, lethargic - but attractive, fish. It will remain motionless in its hiding place for hours at a time and derives its only inspiration from food. Although it lacks motivation other than hunger, it seems constantly hungry; it is amazingly energetic and aggressive when the dinner bell rings. Although peaceful in nature, it nevertheless has a strong tendency to eat anything which will fit in its mouth, so it might be said that it is only truly compatible with fish to large to be considered edible.

Compatible fish: Any fish bigger than bite-size yet no larger than about four times the size of the Raphael

17. **Catfish, Shovelnose**   *Sorubim lima*

Middle-to-bottom swimmer; single fish; egg-layer; not bred in captivity

Often peaceful in the daytime, at night this carnivore will eat any other fish it can fit in its mouth. Although it will get along with other fish, its rapid growth puts sufficient demand upon available space that it is best kept one to a tank.

Compatible fish: #16, #18, #66; and pair fish #10, #15, #23, #25, #42, #44, #45, #47, #51, #57, #63, #71, #77

18. **Catfish, Synodontis** ("Sin-Oh-Don-Tis")   *(many species)*
entire family

Bottom swimmer; egg-layer; most species not bred in captivity

This is a bottom fish, or scavenger. It is a hiding fish and needs places to hide. It also tends to be nocturnal. It has a distinctive face which appears to be encased in armor. One member of the group is known as the "upside- down" fish and always swims belly-up. Almost all Synodontis swim upside-down when very young, but only one variety retains this peculiar swimming manner throughout its lifetime. This lifetime upside-down swimmer is not easily distinguished from its flip-over cousins. Although peaceful in nature, it nevertheless has a strong tendency to eat anything which will fit in its mouth, so one might say that it is compatible only with fish larger than edible.

Compatible fish: Sometimes timid when smaller, and much larger, aggressive fish can intimidate it sufficiently that it will not eat. When larger, however usually will co- exist with almost any fish - including the fierce African Cichlid. As is true with other members of the catfish family, it will swallow whatever will fit in its mouth.

19. **Catfish, Whiptail**   *Loricaria filamentosa*

All-depths swimmer; single fish; egg-layer; bred in captivity

This is an algae-eating fish with sucking-type mouth. It is long and slim and closely resembles a stick. The name arises from the fan-like tip of the tail which snaps back and forth in whip-like fashion as the fish moves from algae source to algae source.

Compatible fish: #9, #16, #37, #66; and school fish #49, #53, #64, #80, #84, #86, #89, #90, #92, #93, #95, #97, #98; and pair fish #35, #36, #58, #59

20. **Cichlid, African** ("Sick-Lid")   *(many families)*
entire group

Bottom-to-middle swimmer; pair fish; egg-layer and usually a mouth-breeder; many species are commonly bred in captivity

There are many beautiful varieties of African Cichlids and they are easily bred. They are, however, extremely territorial and should be kept only with other African Cichlids and perhaps an occasional Synodontis Catfish. Most are too aggressive to go into South American Cichlid tanks; however, sometimes a small African will fit into a community of Cichlids other than African Cichlids. They are diggers and gravel movers. The more caves provided, the more Africans you can keep.

21. **Cichlid, Convict** ("Sick-Lid")   *Cichlastoma nigrofasciatum*

Bottom-to-middle swimmer; pair fish; egg-layer; commonly bred in captivity

These are South American Cichlids. The most common Convicts are noted for their jailhouse-like stripes. These industrious construction workers will dig out and move gravel around to make hiding nests. Light weight tank decorations will not long survive their excavations. These egg-layers breed readily in a home tank but often become very territorially

75

aggressive when breeding. When ready for breeding the female displays a rosy color. These Cichlids are very aggressive and territorial and should only be with other South American Cichlids of the same size; it is best to provide for territories in a Cichlid tank.

Compatible fish: #16, #66; and pair fish #15, #22, #29, #60, #71 - provided that the newcomer is slightly larger than the established residents; and pair fish #10, #20 if they are smaller than the Convict.

22. **Cichlid, Firemouth** ("Sick-Lid")   *Cichlastoma meeki*

Bottom-to-middle swimmer; pair fish; egg-layer; commonly bred in captivity

These South American fish have bright red coloring on the edges of their gills and mouths. They can thrust the gills out in display, and will lock lips with other firemouths also in assertion of territoriality. Cichlids are aggressive and territorial and should only be with other aggressive fish of the same size; it is best to provide for territories in a Cichlid tank. They are gravel excavators and movers.

Compatible fish: #16, #66; and pair fish #21, #29, #30; and pair fish #15, #31 - provided that the newcomer is slightly larger than the established residents; and pair fish #10 & #20 if they are *smaller* than the Firemouth.

23. **Cichlid, Flag** ("Sick-Lid")   *Cichlasoma festivum*

Middle-to-bottom swimmer; pair fish; egg-layer; commonly bred in captivity

Less aggressive than most Cichlids, these are olive in color with a black stripe running from the eye to the end of the dorsal fin. Their fin configuration resembles that the Gourami. Good tank mates for a moderately aggressive community.

Compatible fish: #1, #16, #66; and no more than one of either #73, #75, or #76; and school fish #8, #32, #67; and pair fish #10, #15, #25,

#39, #42, #43, #46, #51, #54, #56, #57, #60, #63, #72

24. **Cichlid, Jack Dempsey** ("Sick-Lid") *Cichlasoma octofasciatum*

Middle-to-bottom swimmer; pair fish; egg-layer; commonly bred in captivity

These are popular, beautiful fish with torquoise-speckled fins. They are very aggressive, can destroy fish larger than they are, and are destructive of tank ornaments. They are sufficiently hostile that it is not uncommon to find one of these as the last survivor in residence.

Compatible fish: #16; and #27 or #28 provided that they are smaller; and #66 provided that it is larger; and pair fish #21, #22, #29 provided that they are equal in size or larger; and pair fish #31 provided that they are smaller

25. **Cichlid, Keyhole** ("Sick-Lid")   *Aequidens maroni*

Middle-to-bottom swimmer; pair fish; egg-layer; commonly bred in captivity

These are among the more peaceful Cichlids and usually do not bother other members of the community. The name arises from a key-hole shaped marking on the body. They are not as disruptive of tank decorations as many of the other Cichlids.

Compatible fish: #1, #16, #18, #66; and no more than one of either #73, #75 or #76; and school fish #8, #32, #67; and pair fish #15, #23, #39, #42, #43, #46, #51, #54, #60, #63

26. **Cichlid, Oscar** ("Sick-Lid")   *Astronotus ocellatus*

All-depths swimmer; single fish; egg-layer; bred in captivity

This is an interesting, very active, personable - if not overly bright - South American fish pet. It grows extremely fast and its large size makes it a threat to all manner of tank decoration. A big eater, it is also a big dispenser of fish waste. Its puppy-like enthusiasm for food generates bull-in-the-china-closet activity at dinner time. Although not by temperament aggressive, the Oscar Cichlid's large size and energetic pursuit of sustenance makes it a threat to tankmates. This fish should not be kept with anything small enough for it to consume. When small, however, anything of equal size (except Catfish with a very small mouth) becomes a threat to this docile youngster.

27. **Cichlid, Pike** ("Sick-Lid") *Crenicichla lepidota*

Bottom swimmer; single fish; egg-layer; bred in captivity

This is a bright, beautifully colored predator but so aggressively territorial that only larger fish can co- exist. It is an incessant digger who will completely disrupt tank decorations and undergravel filter beds as well.

Compatible fish: Catfish of equal or larger size are the best hope for tank mates to this voracious carnivore

28. **Cichlid, Red Devil** (Sick-Lid") *Cichlasoma labiatum*

All-depths swimmer; single fish; egg-layer; bred in captivity

Dull in color when young, the male takes on bright red at sexual maturity. Tank-mates should be chosen very carefully because this is an extremely aggressive fish. It should be kept only with much larger fish of an aggressive nature. The male, in particular, displays very large lip formations. This fish is subject to considerable genetic variation and not all inherit the over-sized lip protrusions.

Compatible fish: provided that *all* are of equal or larger size - #16, #18, #66; and pair fish #24, #31

29. **Cichlid, Red Jewel** ("Sick-Lid") *Hemichromis bimaculatus*

Bottom-to-middle swimmer; pair fish; egg-layer; commonly bred in captivity

South American Red Jewels are narrow-bodied fish and when in color, are very beautiful fish. When not in color they are an uninteresting shade of pale orange. The name comes from sparsely placed, small red scales which are a green iridescent color making the body appear bejeweled. **They are diggers but not so dedicated as other Cichlids.** Red Jewels are aggressive and territorial and should only be with other aggressive fish of the same size; it is best to provide for territories in their tanks.

Compatible fish: #16, #66; and pair fish #21, #22; and pair fish #15, #31 - provided that the newcomer is slightly larger than the established residents; and pair fish #10, & #20 if they are *smaller* than the Red Jewel.

30. **Cichlid, Severum** ("Sick-Lid""Sev-Rum")   *Cichlasoma severum*

All-depth swimmer; pair fish; egg-layer; **bred in captivity**

These are fairly peaceful Cichlids which can **attain great size.** Because of this large size they should not be placed **with very** small fish. Colors will vary considerably from grey-black **stripe** to solid gold or albino. They tend to be aggressive only **when** paired-off and in spawning condition.

Compatible fish: #16, #18, #66; and no more than one of either #73, #75 or #76; and school fish #8, #32, #67; and pair fish #10, #15, #23, #42, #45, #47, #51, #54, #56, #57, #71, #72, #77

31. **Cichlid, Texas** ("Sick-Lid")   *Cichlasoma cyanoguttatum*

Middle-to-bottom swimmer; pair fish; egg-layer; commonly bred in captivity

These are very aggressive fish which grow to large size. They feature very large splotches of turquoise uniformly distributed on their bodies. They are extremely territorial and require much room. They can only be kept with large fish of aggressive nature and in a large tank. They are destructive of tank ornaments.

Compatible fish: Provided that *all* are equal or larger in size - #18, #66; and pair fish #24, #28

32. **Danio, Giant** ("Dan-Yo")   *Danio aequipinnatus*

Surface swimmer; school fish; egg-layer; commonly bred in captivity

These are the largest of the Danio family and can be nippy if deprived of the company of others of their species. They are sturdy, durable fish and, because of their speed and agility, they escape many aggressive attacks. They are seldom caught by other fish and are even difficult to net. They are voracious eaters. They are an iridescent grey or blue color. They are fast enough and large enough not to be bothered by most other fish. If the tank is uncovered, they will exit over the side.

Compatible fish: #1, #66; and no more than one of either #73, #75 or #76; and school fish #6, #7, #8, #67, #97; and pair fish #10, #12, #23, #25, #39, #42, #43, #45, #46, #59, #54, #72

33. **Danio, Pearl** ("Dan-Yo")   *Brachydanio albolineatus*

Surface swimmer; school fish; egg-layer; commonly bred in captivity

These fish remain small (generally under 2 inches in captivity). The name "Pearl" derives from a pearlescent, light-reflective, Abalone-like coloration. When kept in schools of their own species they tend to be fairly peaceful community members. They are fast moving darters and will create action in the tank. When not in schools they can become fin nippers.

Compatible fish: #1, #19, #66; and no more than one of either #73, #75 or #76; and school fish #5, #6, #8, #13, #34, #81, #89, #93; and pair fish #11, #12, #36, #38, #52, #56,,#58

34. **Danio, Zebra** ("Dan-Yo")   *Brachydanio rerio*

Surface swimmer; school fish; egg-layer; bred in captivity

If not in schools they are active fin nippers. These are not very large fish but sufficiently fast enough to elude most pursuers.

They are attractive, inexpensive and popular - with fine gold striping from face to tail. The striping augments a visual impression of great speed. Albino traits and long-fin appendages have been bred into some varieties of the Zebra.

Compatible fish: #1, #19, #66; and no more than one of either #73, #75 or #76; and school fish #5, #6, #8, #13, #33, #81, #89, #93; and pair fish #11, #12, #36, #38, #52, #56, #58

35. **Discus**   **species** *Symphysodon aequifasciata*

All-depths swimmer; pair fish; egg-layer; bred in captivity

One of the most beautiful and appealing tropical freshwaters. Very peaceful but picky eaters, they do not eat well if there is competition for food. They are difficult to keep alive and not recommended for pre- nitrification cycle tanks because of high sensitivity to water chemistry. The best chance of success is probably to wait until the tank is chemically established, then remove the initial tank population and introduce the Discus pairs as the only inhabitants for a period of time. The more there are, the less likely they are to keep out of view.

Compatible fish: #37, #66; and school fish #13, #49, #53, #64, #80, #86, #90, #92, #96; and pair fish #12, #36, #56, #58, #59, #62

36. **Eel, Peacock**   *Macrognathus siamensis*

Bottom swimmer; pair fish; egg-layer; not commonly bred in captivity

These eels like to bury themselves in the finer gravel with only the proboscis visible. The name derives from peacock eye-like markings on the tail. They prefer bloodworms or tubiflex worms for food. They are basically nocturnal in activities and need a very peaceful community as they are reluctant to compete for food.

Compatible fish: #37, #66; and school fish #4, #5, #33, #34, #69, #81, #82, #89, #90, #93, #98; and pair fish #11, #50, #55, #62, #72,

37. **Elephant Nose**   *Gnathonemus petersi*

Bottom swimmer; single fish; egg-layer; not bred in captivity

What appears to be a long nose might be better thought of as an elongated chin. The mouth of the Elephant Nose is above it rather than below it. This leads to a confusing impression that it eats from above its nose. It is easily recognized by the prominent protrusion. This is a hiding fish which appreciates cover and will need a tank well decorated with plants and ornaments to thrive. A very interesting nocturnal fish, it is timid about eating and highly selective about its diet. Two or three weeks will be required for adjustment to new surroundings. It usually can be induced to accept a clear plastic tube open at both ends as a hiding place which it will use in Ostrich-like fashion.

Compatible fish: Provided that they are too large for the Elephant Nose to eat #19, #66; and no more than one of either #73, #75 or #76; and school fish #4, #33, #34, #53 #69, #87, #89, #93; and pair fish #11, #12, #13, #36, #56, #57, #59, #61, #65, #74, #78, #99, #72

38. **Goby, Bumblebee** ("Go-Bee")   *Brachygobius doriae*

Bottom-to-middle swimmer; pair fish; egg-layer; bred in captivity

The name arises because of the black and yellow, bumblebee-like striping. These fish have a tendency to fin nip. They swim in a sort of hopping or bounding fashion and tend to remain in one place for a while, then hop to another. There is a fin under the chin which they often appear to use as a head support by resting the fin on the bottom or on some object.

Compatible fish: #66; and school fish #4, #5, #81, #82, #87, #89, #93, #95, #98; and pair fish #50, #57, #58, #59, #61, #62, #65, #78, #99

39. **Gourami, Blue** ("Go-Ram-Ee") *Trichogaster trichopterus (var.)*

Middle swimmer; pair fish; egg-layer; commonly bred in captivity

These are some of the more aggressive members of the Gourami family. They are sometimes called "two-spot" Gourami. On each side they display a dark blue or black spot mid-body and another at the beginning of the tail. All Gouramis except the Kissing Gourami have a pair of fins under their bodies over which they have surprising control. The long, almost body-length fins, originate under the gills and are used somewhat like feelers; these can be projected in any direction. These fish are fairly aggressive and should be kept with fish the same size or larger.

Compatible fish: #1, #16, #18, #66; and no more than one of either #73, #75 or #76; and school fish #7, #32, #67; and pair fish #10, #23, #42, #43, #46, #57, #63, #60

40. **Gourami, Dwarf** ("Go-Ram-Ee") *Colisa lalia*

Middle swimmer; pair fish; egg-layer; bred in captivity .

These are the most common of the dwarf Gouramis. The distinctive girdled striping of the male makes him significantly more striking than the female. These fish should be kept in pairs because they can become very timid when alone among larger fish. They like to stay well submerged in the tank and dodge in and out of cover and hiding places. All Gouramis except the Kissing Gourami have a pair of fins under their bodies over which they have surprising control. The long, almost body- length, fins originate under the gills and are used somewhat like feelers; these can be projected in any direction.

Compatible fish: #16; and school fish #6, #67, #69, #97, #98; and pair fish #11, #15, #41, #47, #51, #54, #55, #72

41. **Gourami, Dwarf Flame** ("Go-Ram-Ee") *Colisa lalia (var.)*

Bottom-to-middle swimmer; pair fish; egg-layer; commonly bred in captivity

These are more red than other dwarf Gouramis. The males are far more brilliant in color. Among the less aggressive Gouramis, they usually attack only something much smaller. They are shy if not in pairs and should be provided with plenty of plant cover. New surroundings may require a week or so of adjustment. All Gouramis except the Kissing Gourami have a pair of fins under their bodies over which they have surprising control. The long, almost body-length, fins originate under the gills and are used somewhat like feelers; these can be projected in any direction.

Compatible fish: #16, #66; and school fish #6, #67, #69; #97, and pair fish #15, #44, #47, #54, #52, #54, #55, #72

42. **Gourami, Giant** ("Go-Ram-Ee")   *Colisa fasciata*

Bottom-to-middle swimmer; pair fish; egg-layer; commonly bred in captivity

Typically in pet shops these are not noticeably larger than some of the other Gouramis, although in municipal aquariums they can become huge. Although they can be aggressive, these fish tend to be a bit nicer than other of the larger Gouramis but do better when kept in pairs. All Gouramis except the Kissing Gourami have a pair of fins under their bodies over which they have surprising control. The long, almost body-length, fins originate under the gills and are used somewhat like feelers; these can be projected in any direction.

Compatible fish: #1, #16, #18, #17, #66; and no more than one of either #73, #75 or #76; and school fish #7, #32, #67; and pair fish #10, #23, #25, #39, #43, #45, #46, #57, #63, #60, #77

43. **Gourami, Gold** ("Go-Ram-Ee") *Trichogaster trichopterus (var.)*

Middle swimmer; pair fish; egg-layer; commonly bred in captivity

Of the more aggressive Gouramis, like the Blue Gouramis this fish should have tankmates its size or larger because it will bully what it can. The male is a deeper gold than the female and both display intermittent gray shadowing. All Gouramis except the Kissing Gourami have a pair of fins under their bodies over which they have surprising control. The long, almost body-length, fins originate under the gills and are used somewhat like feelers; these can be projected in any direction.

Compatible fish: #1, #16, #18, #17, #66; and no more than one of either #73, #75 or #76; and school fish #7, #32, #67; and pair fish #10, #23, #25, #39, #42, #45, #46, #57, #63, #54, #60

44. Gourami, Kissing ("Go-Ram-Ee")   *Helostoma temmincki*

Middle-to-surface swimmer; pair fish; egg-layer; not easily bred in captivity

The most common is the pink "Kisser"; those procured from the wild are generally green. These are a popular aquarium fish because they are peaceful, easily stand out, and exhibit the peculiar kissing behavior. Only the males use their large mouths to "kiss" each other. Among the Gouramis, only the Kissing Gourami lack the characteristic pair of highly maneuverable fins under their bodies. These relatively calm Gourami usually squabble only with their own kind. Because they attain some size, it is best to get them small.

Compatible fish: #16, #66; and school fish #6, #67, #69; and pair fish #11, #15, #40, #41, #47, #54, #58, #71, #72

45. Gourami, Moonlight ("Go-Ram-Ee")   *Trichogaster microlepis*

Middle-to-surface swimmer; pair fish; egg-layer; bred in captivity

Their entire bodies and finnage are silver with a slight gold tint - somewhat like tarnished silver. They are more aggressive than the Dwarfs and Kissing Gouramis but less aggressive than the Blue, Opaline or Gold. Although they attain considerable size, because they are not particularly aggressive they do not threaten many of the fish less large. All Gouramis except the Kissing Gourami have a pair of fins under their bodies over which they have surprising control. The long, almost body- length, fins originate under the gills and are used somewhat like feelers and can be projected in any direction.

Compatible fish: #16, #17, #66; and school fish #6, #67, #69; and pair fish #15, #23, #25, #40, #42, #44, #47, #51, #60, #77

46. **Gourami, Opaline** ("Go-Ram-Ee")("Oh-Pa-Line")
Trichogaster trichopterus (var.)

Bottom-to-middle swimmer; pair fish; egg-layer, commonly bred in captivity

Similar to the Blue Gourami in both appearance and behavior but without the Blue Gourami's dots, these are aggressive and should be kept with fish the same size or larger. All Gouramis except the Kissing Gourami have a pair of fins under their bodies over which they have surprising control. The long, almost body-length, fins originate under the gills and are used somewhat like feelers and can be projected in any direction.

Compatible fish: #1, #16, #18, #17, #66; and no more than one of either #73, #75 or #76; and school fish #7, #32, #67; and pair fish #10, #39, #30, #42, #43, #45, #57, #63, #54, #60

47. **Gourami, Pearl Leeri** ("Go-Ram-Ee")("Leer-Ree")
Trichogaster leeri

Middle-to-surface swimmer; pair fish; egg-layer; bred in captivity

Of the Gouramis, these are among the more peaceful. They are not as aggressive as the Opaline, Gold or Blue but slightly more aggressive than the dwarf variations. It is best to get them small so that they grow up in the community. All Gouramis except the Kissing Gourami have a pair of fins under their bodies over which they have surprising control. The long, almost body-length, fins originate under the gills and are used somewhat like feelers; these can be projected in any direction.

Compatible fish: #16, #66; and school fish #6, #67, #69, #97; and pair fish #11, #15, #40, #41, #42, #44, #45, #46, #47, #55, #72, #77,

86

48. **Guppies** ("Guh-Pees")   *Poecilia reticulata*
    entire group

All-depth swimmer; pair fish; live-bearer; commonly bred in captivity

There are many species of Guppies, but they must be in a peaceful tank because many fish will eat their fancy and beautiful tails. The more beautiful their tails, the more susceptible they are to fin-nibbler attack. They breed easily in home aquariums, either intentionally or haphazardly. Ample plants and vegetation in the tank will give baby Guppies a better chance of survival.

Compatible fish: #66; and school fish #14, #49, #70, #85, #88, #91, #64, #79, #84, #94; and pair fish #59, #62

49. **Hatchet Fish, Silver**   *Gasteropelecus sternicla*

Surface swimmer; school fish; egg-layer; not easily bred in captivity

Once seen, their distinctive body shape is unmistakable and gives rise to their name. These fish are similar to flying fish and are so prone to hopping out of an uncovered tank as to suggest a strong inclination to fly. Tanks should have a tight top. These fish are either solid silver or marbled with black.

Compatible fish: #19, #66; and school fish #14, #70, #85, #88, #91, #68, #79, #86, #94; and pair fish #48, #59, #50

50. **Killies** ("Kill-Lees")   *Aphyosemion*

Surface swimmer; pair fish; egg-layers; most species commonly bred in captivity

These vary greatly in color. They tend to jump out of the tank. They remain small but get along fairly well with other peaceful community members.

Compatible fish: #19, #66; and school fish #4, #81, #82, #87, #89, #93, #95; and pair fish #12,

#38, #56, #58, #59, #61, #62, #65, #78, #99

51. **Knife, Clown**   *Notopterus chitala*

Middle-to-bottom swimmer; pair fish; egg-layer; not easily bred in captivity

As do all knife fish, these have a single fin underneath the body. These are hiding fish which appreciate cover and to thrive will want a tank with many plants or ornaments. They are peaceful fish and can live with most any fish too large to eat. Although not bullies, in an uncrowded tank they grow very quickly and their capacity to devour increases accordingly. They co-exist well with whatever fish are too large, too fast or too frightening for them to eat.

52. **Knife, Ghost**   *Apteronotus albifrons*

Bottom-to-middle swimmer; pair fish; egg-layer; not bred in captivity

As do all knife fish, these have a single fin underneath the body. These are hiding fish and require safe hiding places to feel at home. There must be at least one hideout per Knife. They are nocturnal and prefer frozen foods. They can live with most any fish which they cannot eat. Although all Knifes give off a minor electric current for defense, the Ghost Knife emits the strongest current. Except for extremely aggressive fish, these will get along well with whatever they cannot eat.

Compatible fish: #3, #16, #37, #66; and school fish #5, #6, #33, #34, #69, #81, #82, #89, #93; and pair fish #12, #40, #41, #44, #45, #47, #55, #74, #58, #72

53. **Knife, Glass**   *Eigenmannia virescens*

Middle swimmer; school fish; egg-layer; not bred in captivity

As do all knife fish, these have a single fin underneath the body. These are timid, tiny-mouthed fish which are fascinating because they are transparent. The skeletal and muscular structure are visible. They require a very clean tank and considerable plastic or real vegetation to hide in. They tend to prefer frozen foods.

Compatible fish: #19, #66; and school fish #4, #14, #33, #34, #49, #82, #87, #89, #93, #79, #84, #94; and pair fish #12, #59, #61, #65, #50, #99

54. **Kribensis** ("Crib-Ben-Sis")   *Pelvicachromis pulcher*

Bottom-to-middle swimmer; pair fish; egg-layer; commonly bred in captivity

These are dwarf Cichlids. One of the few Cichlids which feature a female far prettier than the male. When the females are in breeding color, they are beautifully colorful and display a purplish violet belly and yellow or brown and gold stripes. Somewhat territorial, they manage to get along fairly well with other somewhat aggressive fish.

Compatible fish: #1, #66; and no more than one of either #73, #75 or #76; and school fish #7, #8, #32, #33, #34, #67, #82, #95; and pair fish #12, #23, #30, #42, #45, #47, #52, #56, #57, #58, #60, #71, #72

55. **Leaf Fish**   *Monocirrhus polyacantus*

Surface swimmer; pair fish; egg-layer; bred in captivity

These fish bear a striking resemblance to a leaf from a tree. Like a floating leaf, these flat fish lurk motionless at the surface of the water stalking prey. They prefer some surface cover. When swimming their fins move so rapidly as to be almost invisible; but, unless striking at prey, they move through the water surely and steadily in fashion reminiscent of a moving submarine.

Compatible fish: #16, #19, #37, #66; and school fish #4, #5, #80, #81, #82, #86, #87, #89, #93, #96, #97, #98

56. **Loach, Clown**   *Botia macrocantha*

Bottom swimmer; pair fish; egg-layer; not bred in captivity

These are truly the tank clowns. They will lie on their sides and "play dead" on the tank floor or on decorations. They will swim on their sides, up-side down, and "every which way". During feeding they often emit loud clicking noises. They are hiding fish; they like to be in groups of 2 or more, and they need cover. They have a spear-like spine on either side of the face, originating at the mouth. The spines are normally not visible but can be extended for defense against larger, more aggressive fish.

Compatible fish: #16, #19, #66; and no more than one of either #73, #75 or #76; and school fish #4, #6, #13, #33, #34, #67, #69, #87, #89, #93; and pair fish, #11, #12, #15, #40, #41, #44, #47, #52, #57, #59, #61, #65, #54, #74, #78, #99, #71, #72

57. Loach, Dojo (Weather)   *Misgurnus anguillicaudatus*

Bottom swimmer; pair fish; egg-layer; nor bred in captivity

These are scavenger fish which like to hide under rock or log decorations. They are, nevertheless, friendly fish who will come out more if there are others in the tank. They are sandy colored with a snake-like shape. These fish will get along with any fish that won't eat them. With a sort of "hang-dog" appearance and manner these fish vaguely remind one of bloodhounds.

Compatible fish: #16, #66; and no more than one of either #73, #75 or #76; and school fish #6, #7, #8, #32, #33, #34, #81, #82, #89, #93; and pair fish #2, #11, #40, #41, #44 #45 , #47, #55, #78, #72, #77; and pair fish #61, #65 if too large to be eaten by the Dojo (Weather) Loach.

58. Loach, Horseface   *Acanthopsis choirorhynchus*

Bottom swimmer; pair fish; egg-layer; not commonly bred in captivity

A horse's face they have, indeed! These are very peaceful scavenger fish. They like to bury themselves in the gravel. They are a sandy brown color displaying a checkerboard pattern on their backs. They tend to be nocturnal.

Compatible fish: #1, #66; and no more than one of either #73, #75 or #76; and school fish #4, #5, #6, #7, #32, #33, #34, #64, #68, #69, #81, #87, #89, #93, #95, #96, #97, #98; and pair fish #12, #40, #41, #50, #56, #57, #72

59. Loach, Kuhli ("Kool-Lee")   *Acanthopthalmus kuhli*

Bottom swimmer, pair fish; egg-layer; some members have been bred in captivity

These are extremely fast, colorful fish and often playful with their paired partner. They have a pencil-thin body ringed with orange and black stripes. They are scavenger fish and hiding fish, and fare best in a well decorated tank.

Compatible fish: #19, #37, #66; and school fish #4, #5, #14, #33, #34, #69, #70, #81, #82, #85, #87, #88, #89, #91, #93, #100, #64, #80, #86, #90, #95, #96, #97, #98; and pair fish #12, #61, #65, #78, #99

60. Loach, Yo-yo   *Botia lochata*

Bottom-to-middle swimmer; pair fish; egg-layer; not commonly bred in captivity

These are somewhat quarrelsome members of the Bottia family and like other Bottias have recessed facial spines which can be extended and used for defense. They are fairly aggressive and should not be kept with tiny peaceful fish. It is often possible to discern audible clicking. Their markings feature discontinuous but tiger-like striping, intermittent gold and brown.

Compatible fish: #1, #17, #66; and no more than one of either #73, #75 or #76; and school fish #8, #32, #67; and pair fish #10, #15, #23, #25, #30, #39, #42, #43, #46, #57, #63, #72

61. **Mollies** (Moll-lees)   *Poeciliai*
    entire family

All-depths swimmer; pair fish; live-bearer; commonly bred in captivity

These fish come in a variety of colors, sizes and finnage. They multiply rapidly in aquariums. They will eat vegetation and like to have some vegetable matter present to snack on. They prefer water to which a small amount of un-iodized salt has been added.

Compatible fish: #66; and school fish #4, #5, #13, #38, #81, #82, #89, #93; and pair fish #12, #56, #57, #59, #61, #65, #50, #74, #78, #58, #99

62. **Otocinclus** ("Oh-Toe-Sink-Lus")   *Otocinclus mariae*

All-depth swimmer; pair fish; egg-layer; bred in captivity

These are an extremely peaceful, algae-eating fish which will not harm other plants. They remain small and do not harm other fish. They are ideal for a peaceful tank such as a Neon or Guppy tank.

Compatible fish: School fish #4, #5, #6, #13, #14, #49, #53, #64, #70, #79, #84, #85, #88, #91, #94; and pair fish #50, #59, #61, #65, #78, #99

63. **Paradise Fish**   *Macropodus opercularis*

Bottom-to-middle swimmer; pair fish; egg-layer; commonly bred in captivity

These are among the more aggressive members of the Gourami family; When in breeding color, they are beautiful. They are extremely territorial and capable of defending themselves against many larger fish. The fins under the gills and mouth are more conventionally shaped and less like feelers than those of the other members of the Gourami family.

Compatible fish: #1, #16, #18, #66; and no more than one of either #73, #75 or #76; and school fish, #7, #32, #67; and pair fish #10, #42, #43, #46, #57, #60

64. **Pencilfish**   *Nannostomus unifasciatus*

Surface swimmer; school fish; egg-layer; bred in captivity

These fish are given to the peculiar behavior pattern of "hanging" in schools at the surface of the water with faces turned upward. They are timid fish and tend to avoid the center area of the aquarium. They are small- mouthed fish able to eat only small morsels; and, they prefer floating food.

Compatible fish: #66; and school fish #13, #49, #53, #81, #82, #87, #89, #90, #93, #96, #97, #98; and pair fish #12, #36, #59, #65, #99

65. **Platies** ("Plat-Tees")   *Xiphophorus maculatus*
entire group

All-depths swimmer; pair fish; live-bearers; commonly bred in captivity.

These fish tend to be a bit smaller than most common live-bearers. Some beautiful hybrid members have exceptionally high fins. There are many different colors and kinds. They are best kept in pairs of 2 females to 1 male.

Compatible fish: #19, #66; and school fish #4, #13, #64, #86, #92; and pair fish #12, #56, #57, #59, #61, #50, #78, #99; and pair fish #74 if no more than 4 times as large as the Platies

66. **Plecostomus** ("Pleck-Ost-Oh-Mus")   *Hypostomus plecostomus*

Bottom and side swimmer; single fish; egg-laying; not commonly bred in captivity

This is a peaceful, nocturnal resident that feeds on algae. It should not be added to the tank until algae is visible. If this fish is very large or if there are too many of these "Plecos", a food shortage may arise. Some members of this group have extremely hard, rasp-like teeth capable of scratching acrylic tanks. This fish will get along with whatever will not eat it but can develop stress in the presence of other algae-eating fish if their common food supply (algae) becomes inadequate. While, on occasion, it will eat another fish, the fish consumed is inevitably a fish that was already dead or dying.

67. **Rainbow Fish**   *Melanotaenia*

Middle-to-surface swimmer; school fish; egg-layer; most members bred in captivity

These are fast, surface schooling fish. There are many, many colorful members of this group - some quite difficult for stores to obtain. Their colors are most striking when there are more males than females. If these are in groups of 4 or more they rarely give any compatibility problems.

Compatible fish: #16, #18, #66; and no more than one of either #73, #75 or #76; and school fish #6, #32, #67, #69, #87, #81, #82, #89 #93; and pair fish #12, #15, #23, #25, #40, #41, #30, #44, #45, #47, #52, #56, #54, #72, #77

68. **Ram**   *Apistogramma ramirezi*

Bottom-to-middle swimmer; school fish; egg-layer; bred in captivity

These are brightly colored fish in many variations - the most common being gold with blue and/or red. The are very particular about water chemistry. They are timid and will not withstand much feeding competition.

Compatible fish: #37, #66; and school fish #4, #5, #13, #33, #34, #69, #81, #87, #89, #93, #95, #98; and pair fish #12, #36, #55, #56, #58, #59, #72

69. **Rasbora, Brilliant** ("Ras-Bore-Ah")   *Rasbora steineri*

Middle-to-surface swimming; school fish; egg-laying; not bred in captivity

These fish must be in schools and will dart back and forth in the top third of the tank. These peaceful, lively fish will keep a tank in motion. Do not leave the tank uncovered; they are very likely to jump out.

Compatible fish: #66; and no more than one of either #73, #75 or $76; and school fish #4, #5, #13, #33, #34, #53, #81, #82, #87, #89, #93, #97, #98; and pair fish #12, #36, #38, #56, #59, #61, #55, #58, #78, #99, #72

70. **Rasbora, Hetermorpha** ("Ras-Bore-Ah") *Rasbora hetermorpha*

Middle swimmer; school fish; egg-layer; bred in captivity

These are very pretty, copper colored fish with a black triangle on the body pointing toward the tail. They are very peaceful. In the presence of other fish which are zealous feeders, these fish can become timid at feeding time and may be left out.

Compatible fish: #66; and school fish #14, #49, #59, #88, #85, #64, #91, #100, #79, #84, #94; and pair fish #12, #48, #59

71. **Ropefish**   *Calamoichthys calabaricus*

Bottom swimmer; pair fish; egg-layer; not bred in captivity

These are so called because they resemble a tightly braided rope. They are not colorful. They are peaceful, hiding fish and not aggressive. They prefer frozen food and can not have much competition for food. If subjected to much aggression, they are likely to elect over-the- side suicide. Truly healthy specimens are sometimes in short supply.

Compatible fish: #1, #66; and no more than one of either #73, #75 or #76; and school fish #6, #7, #8, #32, #67; and pair fish #15, #30, #44, #45, #47, #51, #52, #57, #72, #74, #77

72. **Shark, Bala** ("Bah-Lah" or "Bay-Lah")
                                    Balantiocheilos melanopterus

Middle-to-surface swimmer; pair fish; egg-layer; not bred in captivity

These are aluminum foil colored and show off best against a dark background tank. They are fond of eating vegetation. Unlike most sharks, it is not necessary to limit them one to a tank because they are not as aggressive as most other sharks. They actually get along well with fish of their own size.

Compatible fish: #16, #37, #66; and school fish #8, #32, #33, #34, #67, #69, #81, #93, #95; and pair fish #12, #36, #40, #41, #52, #55, #56, #57, #59, #71

73. **Shark, Black**   *Labeo forskazi*

Bottom-to-middle swimmer; single fish; egg-layer; not easily bred in captivity

This fish can be a fin nipper. Because it is extremely territorial, it is best that it be the only shark, of any kind, in the tank; and unless the tank population is unusually aggressive, best to have the shark slightly smaller than the other fish. Black Sharks seem to grow faster and larger in captivity than other sharks.

Compatible fish: 66; and school fish #7, #8, #32; and pair fish #12, #15, #23, #25, #39, #42, #30, #43, #45, 46, #56, #63, #60

74. **Shark, Iridescent**   *Pangasius sutchi*

Bottom swimmer; pair fish; egg-layer; not easily bred in captivity

As a pair fish, these sharks differ from the other sharks in that these prefer to be with another of their own kind and will thrive better under those conditions. They are hiding fish. When newly introduced to a tank, they can prove timid feeders and they tend to shock rather dramatically upon transfer from one tank to another. In states of shock, they will sometimes appear to be dead. If, however, there are sufficient places to hide in the new tank, they usually snap back readily.

Compatible fish: #19, #66; school fish #6, #8, #32, #33, #34, #69, #81, #82, #89, #93; and pair fish #11, #12, #15, #13, #40, #41, #44,

75. **Shark, Rainbow**   *Labeo erythrurus*

Bottom-to-middle swimmer; single fish; egg-layer; not easily bred in captivity

This fish can be a fin-nipper. Because it is extremely territorial, it is best that it be the only shark, of any kind, in the tank; and unless the tank population is unusually aggressive, best that it be slightly smaller than the other fish. This is a tank-hopper with pronounced suicidal tendencies and will exit if the tank is left uncovered.

Compatible fish: 66; and school fish #7, #8, #32; and pair fish #12, #23, #25, #39, #42, #43, #45, #46, #56, #59, #63, #54, #60, #71; and pair fish #15 if not larger than 2 1/2 times the shark

76. **Shark, Red Tail**   *Labeo bicolor*

Bottom-to-middle swimmer; single fish; egg-layer; not easily bred in captivity

This fish can be a fin nipper. Because it is extremely territorial, it is best that it be the only shark, of any kind, in the tank; and unless the tank population is unusually aggressive, best that it be slightly smaller than the other fish. This is a tank-hopper and will exit if the tank is left uncovered.

Compatible fish: 66; and school fish #7, #8, #32; and pair fish #12, #23, #25, #39, #42, #43, #45, #46, #56, #59, #63, #54, #60; and pair fish #15 if not larger than 2 1/ times the shark

77. **Silver Dollar**   *Metynnis hypsauchen*

Middle-to-surface swimmer; school fish; egg-layer; not commonly bred in captivity

Although not truly so, these are considered "scaleless" fish and are very susceptible to parasitic infections upon transfer.

Precautions should be taken when medication is used because they are not as resistant to chemical burns as most other fish. Peaceful when small, they grow quickly and with size become notably aggressive.

Compatible fish: #1, #16, #18, #66; and school fish #8, #32, #67; and pair fish #10, #15, #30, #44, #51, #52, #56, #57, #71

78. **Swordtails**   *Xiphophorus helleri*

All-depths swimmer; pair fish; live-bearers; commonly bred in captivity

There are many different colors and kinds of these fish and they are best kept in groups of 2 females and 1 male. If paired, a male and female are best. Unlike other live-bearers the males have a sword-like extension from their tails which make them easily distinguishable from the females. These will leap out of an uncovered tank.

Compatible fish: #66; and school fish #4, #13, #81, #87, #89, #80, #90, #96; and school fish #74 provided it is too small to eat the Swordtails; and pair fish #12, #36, #56, #57, #59, #61, #65, #58, #99

79. **Tetra, Black Neon**   *Hyphessobrycon herbertaxelrodi*

Middle swimmer; school fish; egg-layer; not commonly bred in captivity

These are small, gray bodied community fish displaying an iridescent white stripe running from eye to tail set off by a black stripe just below it.

Compatible fish: #19, #66; and school fish #14, #53, #84, #85, #88, #91, #94; and pair fish #12, #48, #59

80. **Tetra, Black Phantom**   *Megalamphodus megalopterus*

All-depth swimmer; school fish; egg-layer; bred in captivity

These are imposing, graceful, medium sized Tetras.

Compatible fish: #19, #66; and school fish #4, #64, #81,
#82, #86, #87, #89, #90, #93, #95, #96,
#97; and pair fish #12, #36, #59, #62

81. **Tetra, Black Skirt**   *Gymnocorymbus ternetzi*

Middle swimmer; school fish; egg-layer; commonly bred in
captivity

These are medium size fish which almost always establish and
maintain a pecking order within their own species. They may
bully much smaller fish. Often the top fish in the pecking order
can be recognized because it will have a bloated appearance
resembling being egg-laden even though it is not.

Compatible fish: #19, #66; and school fish #13, #69, #82,
#87, #89, #93, #100, #80, #86, #90, #92,
#95, #98; and pair fish #12, #40, #41,
#36, #56, #59, #78

82. **Tetra. Bleeding Heart**   *Hyphessobrycon erythrostigma*

Middle swimmer; school fish; egg-layer; commonly bred in
captivity

These are easily identified by long black & white dorsal fins on
red bodies with darker red spots on each side.

Compatible fish: #66; and school fish #13, #53, #69, #81,
#87, #89, #93, #64, #100, #80, #86, #96,
#98; and pair fish #12, #56, #59, #50,
#78

83. **Tetra, Blind Cave**   *Astyanax fasciatus mexicanus*

All-depth swimmer; school fish; egg-layer; bred in captivity

These are not particularly pretty fish but have the unusual
feature of being hatched without eyes and totally blind. They
tend to be nippy in their sightless search for food.

Compatible fish: #1, #16; and school fish #7, #33, #34,
                    #69, #96, #97; and pair fish #12, #40,
                    #41, #44, #56, #57, #58, #59, #72

84. **Tetra, Bloodfin**   *Aphyocharax anisitsi*

Bottom-to-middle swimmer; school fish; egg-layer; bred in
captivity

These are timid little white fish characterized by blood red
finnage and tails. In a very active tank, they may suffer starva-
tion.

Compatible fish: #19, #66; and school fish #14, #49, #53,
                    #64, #70, #79, #85, #88, #91, #94; and
                    pair fish #12, #48, #59, #62

85. **Tetra, Cardinal**   *Cheirodon axelrod*

Bottom-to-middle swimmer; school fish; egg-layer; not easily
bred in captivity

These are bright, neon-like fish with a red stripe running the
entire length of their bodies whereas a true Neon Tetra's stripe
runs only half the length of its body. This is a peaceful fish that
requires good water quality. It is not a good choice for the
initial cycling group in a new tank.

Compatible fish: #66; and school fish #14, #70, #88, #91,
                    #100, #79, #84, #94; and pair fish #12,
                    #48, #49, #59, #62

86. **Tetra, Emperor**   *Inpaichthys kerri*

Middle swimmer; school fish; egg-layer; can be bred in captivity

In appearance these might call to mind Black Neons, but
glorified with much brighter colors. They are easily stressed in
shipping and should be observed carefully for the first few days
after accession.

Compatible fish: #19, #66; and school fish #13, #49, #64,
                    #80, #82, #88, #90, #92, #96, #100; and
                    pair fish #12, #58, #59, #62

87. Tetra, Glass

Chanda ranga

Bottom-to-middle swimmer; school fish; egg-layer; bred in captivity

These are transparent fish which like to hide in vegetation. They are bolder and more visible when there are a large number in the same tank. Dealers sometimes paint the backs of Glass Tetras with fluorescent colors to make them more attractive; however, the paint eventually wears off.

Compatible fish: #19, #66; and school fish #14, #49 #53, #69, #81, #89, #93, #100, #68, #80, #98; and pair fish #12, #38, #56, #59, #38, #78

88. Tetra, Glowlight

Hemigrammus erythrozonus

Bottom-to-middle swimmer; school fish; egg-layer; not commonly bred in captivity

These are peaceful fish. The orange stripes running head to tail on each side appear neon-like under certain lighting.

Compatible fish: #19, #66; and school fish #14, #49, #53, #70, #82, #85, #87, #89, #91, #100, #79, #84, #94; and pair fish #12, #56, #59, #99

89. Tetra, Head & Tail Light

Hemigrammus ocellifer

Middle swimmer; school fish; egg-layer; bred in captivity

These are medium sized schooling fish; they are, in general, very peaceful but will sometimes bully a much smaller fish. As their name implies, they have a red dot over each eye for "headlights" and a yellow-orange dot on each side of the tail for "tail lights".

Compatible fish: #19, #66; and school fish #13, #53, #69, #81, #87 #89, #93, #100, #68, #95, #98; and pair fish #12, #36, #56, #61, #65, #59, #78, #99

90. **Tetra, Lemon**   *Hyphessobrycon pulchripinnis*

Middle swimmer; school fish, egg-layers, bred in captivity

Lemon yellow fish with bright red eyes, they are peaceful in
spite of being among the larger size Tetras. They do well with
other peaceful fish of slightly greater size.

Compatible fish: #19, #66; and school fish #4, #13, #49,
                    #69, #80, #82, #86, #88, #89, #92, #96,
                    #100; and pair fish #12, #50, #58, #59,
                    #65, #78, #99

91. **Tetra, Neon**   *Paracheirodon innesi*

Middle swimmer; school fish; egg-layer; not commonly bred in
captivity

These are among the most popular fishes. They prefer groups
of 4 or more; and, the more there are, the less likely these fish
are to become stressed. Because they are not terribly hardy
fish, they are not a good choice for the initial cycling group in
a new tank.

Compatible fish: #66; and school fish #14, #49, #53, #70,
                    #85, #88, #100, #79, #84, #94; and pair
                    fish #12, #48, #56, #59, #62, #99

92. **Tetra, Penguin**   *Thayeria boehlkei*

Surface swimmer; school fish; egg-layer; bred in captivity

These are silver fish with a black stripe running from the eye
and ending on only the lower half of tailfin. Their swimming
posture makes them appear to be angling upward while swimming horizontally. This appearance is heightened by the
tapering-off black stripe. They are reasonably tranquil, agree-
able fish.

Compatible fish: #19, #66; and school fish #13, #49, #53,
                    #64, #80, #82, #86, #87, #90, #96, #100;
                    and pair fish #12, #59, #62, #99

93. **Tetra, Red Eye**   *Moenkhausia sanctaefilomenae*

Middle-to-upper swimmer; school fish; egg-layer; bred in captivity

These medium sized schooling fish may bully smaller residents. There eyes are circled with a ring of red. They are a fairly fast fish with also a black ring around the tail.

Compatible fish: #66; and school fish #13, #49, #69, #81, #82, #87, #89, #100, #83, #95, #97, #98; and pair fish #12, #36, #56, #59, #61, #65, #78, #58, #99

94. **Tetra, Rummy-Nose**   *Hemigrammus rhodostomus*

Bottom-to-middle swimmer; school fish; egg-laying; not commonly bred in captivity

These are pretty little fish with striking coloration. The face and mouth are bright red fading into a silver body with a black and white striped tail.

Compatible fish: #19, #66; and school fish #14, #49, #53, #70, #79, #84, #85, #88, #91; and pair fish 12, #48, #59

95. **Tetra, Serpae** ("Sir-Pay")   *Hyphessobrycon sepae serpae*

Middle swimmer; school fish; egg-laying; bred in captivity

These are among the slightly more aggressive Tetras. Often when acquired, they tend to be pale in color, but after a few weeks they can become bright red. Six or more are preferable to three because their aggressiveness declines with the larger family.

Compatible fish: #1, #66; and school fish #4, #13, #33, #34, #69, #81, #83, #89, #93, #97, #98; and pair fish #12, #44, #56, #57, #58, #59

96. **Tetra, Scissortail** *Rasbora trilineata*

Surface swimmer; school fish; egg-laying; bred in captivity

These are plain, peaceful fish which derive their name from the scissor-like action of their tails when they swim.

Compatible fish: #19, #66; and school fish #13, #49, #53, #79, #80, #86, #88, #90, #92, #100; and pair fish #12, #58, #59, #61, #62, #65, #78, #99

97. **Tetra, Silvertip** *Hasemania nana*

Surface swimmer; school fish; egg-laying; not bred in captivity

These resemble the Scissortail Tetra except for white tips on upper, lower and tail fins. Their body color is slightly golden. They are fast fish and hard to catch.

Compatible fish: #19, #66; and school fish #4, #64, #68, #69, #81, #87, #89, #93, #95, #98; and pair fish #12, #58, #59, #62

98. **Tetra, Von Rio** *Hyphessobrycon flammeus*

Middle swimmer; school fish; egg-laying; bred in captivity

These are somewhat rounder-shaped Tetra. They are golden colored in the head area fading into red mid-body, and becoming completely red in the tail area.

Compatible fish: #19, #66; and school fish #4, #68, #69, #81, #87, #89, #93, #95, #97; and pair fish #12, #44, #50, #56, #58, #59, #61, #62, #65, #78, #99

99. **Variatus ("Very-Ottus")** *Xiphophorus variatus*

Middle swimmer; pair fish; live-bearer; commonly bred in captivity

There are several different kinds of this fish. They are among the smaller live bearing fish. They like a little vegetation in their diets. They are not likely to jump out of an uncovered tank.

Compatible fish: #19, #66; and school fish #4, #81, #82, #87, #89, #68, #80, #86, #90, #92, #96; and school fish #74 only if Variatus is too large to be eaten by it; and pair fish #11, #12, #38, #56, #57, #59, #61, #65, #50, #78, #58

100. White Cloud Mountain Fish   *Tanichthys albonubes*

Surface swimmer; school fish; egg-layer; commonly bred in captivity

These are hardy, little fish capable of withstanding substantial temperature variation if it occurs slowly.

Compatible fish: #19, #66; and school fish #4, #13, #53, #69, #70, #81, #87, #88, #89, #93, #64, #80, #86, #90, #92, #96, #97; and pair fish #12, #48, #49, #56, #57, #59, #61, #65, #50, #78, #62, #99

- FINDER TWO -

280 COMMON NAME IDENTIFIER

This alphabetical listing includes the 100 numbered fish names from FINDER ONE as well as 180 additional names. The additional names include name variations, other common names, nicknames, and names of similar fish.

You will save time by looking here first - then referring to FINDER ONE.

There are thousands of fresh water tropical fish. FINDER ONE of *THE FISHBUYER'S FISHFINDER* was an extensive but arbitrary selection of names. Similarly, the additional names and nicknames below have been arbitrarily selected simply because I have often heard them used. By listing these name versions I hope to make it easier for readers to locate a fish that they may know by a name different from the names selected numbered in FINDER ONE.

Name	For Compatibility See
Albino Cat	**#12 Catfish, Corydorus**
Albino Iridescent	**#74 Shark, Iridescent**
Algae Eater, Chinese - #1	
Aneus Cat	**#12 Catfish, Corydorus**
Angelfish - #2	
Arowana - #3	
Auratus	**#20 Cichlid, African**
Australian Rainbow	**#67 Rainbow**
Bala	**#72 Shark, Bala**
Barb, Cherry - #4	
Barb, Gold - #5	
Barb, Rosy - #6	
Barb, Tiger - #7	
Barb, Tin Foil - #8	
Bettas - #9	
Black Angelfish	**#2 Angelfish**
Black Angelfish, Half	**#2 Angelfish**
Black Guppy, 3/4	**#48 Guppies**

Black Neon	**#79 Tetra, Black Neon**
Black Swordtail	**#78 Swordtails**
Bloodfin	**#84 Tetra, Bloodfin**
Blue Moon	**#65 Platies**
Blue Paradise	**#63 Paradise**
Blue Platy	**#65 Platies**
Blue Ram	**#68 Ram**
Bosmani Rainbow	**#67 Rainbow**
Botias - #10	
Botia Loachata	**#60 Loach, Yo-yo**
Brichardi	**#20 Cichlid, African**
Bristle Nose	**#66 Plecostomus**
Bumblebee	**#38 Goby, Bumblebee**
Butterfly Fish - #11	
Candy Plecostomus	**#66 Plecostomus**
Candy Swordtail	**#78 Swordtails**
Catfish, Corydorus - #12	
Catfish, Debawi - #13	
Catfish, Glass - #14	
Catfish, Pictus	
Pimolodella - #15	
Catfish, Raphael - #16	
Catfish, Shovelnose - #17	
Catfish, Synodontis - #18	
Catfish, Whiptail - #19	
Celebes Rainbow	**#67 Rainbow**
Cherry Barb	**#4 Barb, Cherry**
Chinese Algae Eater	**#1 Algae Eater, Chinese**
Cichlid, African - #20	
Cichlid, Convict - #21	
Cichlid, Firemouth - #22	
Cichlid, Flag - #23	
Cichlid, Jack Dempsey - #24	
Cichlid, Keyhole - #25	
Cichlid, Oscar - #26	
Cichlid, Pike - #27	
Cichlid, Red Devil - #28	
Cichlid, Red Jewel - #29	
Cichlid, Severum - #30	
Cichlid, Texas - #31	
Cobra Guppy, Red	**#48 Guppies**
Cobra Guppy, Green	**#48 Guppies**
Danio, Giant - #32	
Danio, Pearl - #33	

Danio, Zebra - #34
    Debawi   #13 Catfish,
    Dempsey   #24 Cichlid, Jack Dempsey
Discus - #35
    Dojo Weather Loach   #57 Loach, Dojo Weather
    Dwarf Botias   #10 Botias
    Dwarf Gourami, Honey   #40 Gourami, Dwarf
Eel, Peacock - #36
Elephant Nose - #37
    Elephant Nose Petersi   #37 Elephant Nose
    Fancy Guppy   #48 Guppies
    Feeder Guppy   #48 Guppies
    Festivum   #23 Cichlid, Flag
    Fighting Fish   #9 Bettas
    Firemouth Cichlid   #22 Cichlid, Firemouth
    Flame Tetra   #98 Tetra, Von Rio
    Flamingo Guppy   #48 Guppies
    Four Line Cat   #15 Catfish, Pictus
    Frontosa   #20 Cichlid, African
    German Half-black   #48 Guppies
    Ghost Knife   #52 Knife, Ghost
    Giant Danio   #32 Danio, Giant
    Glass Cat   #14 Catfish, Glass
    Glass Knife   #53 Knife, Glass
Goby, Bumblebee - #38
    Gold Angelfish   #2 Angelfish
    Gold Barb   #5 Barb, Gold
    Gold Platy   #65 Platies
    Gold Moon   #65 Platies
    Gold Ram   #68 Ram
    Gold Tux   #78 Swordtails
    Gold Wag Swordtail   #78 Swordtails
Gourami, Blue - #39
Gourami, Dwarf - #40
Gourami, Dwarf Flame - #41
Gourami, Giant - #42
Gourami, Gold - #43
Gourami, Kissing - #44
Gourami, Moonlight - #45
Gourami, Opaline - #46
Gourami, Pearl Leeri - #47
    Green Iridescent   #74 Shark, Iridescent
    Green Painted Swordtail   #78 Swordtails

Guppies - #48

H & T Tetra	#89 Tetra, Head & Tail Lt.
Haplochromis	#20 Cichlid, African
Harlequin Fish	#70 Rasbora, Heteromorpha
Harlequin Rasbora	#70 Rasbora, Heteromorpha

Hatchet Fish, Silver - #49

Head & Tail Light Tetra	#89 Tetra, Head & Tail Lt.
Hi Fin Swordtail	#78 Swordtails
Honey Dwarf	#40 Gourami, Dwarf
Horseface	#58 Loach, Horseface
Iranian Red	#67 Rainbow
Jack Dempsey	#24 Cichlid, Jack Dempsey
Jewel Cichlid	#29 Cichlid, Red Jewel
Julii	#12 Catfish, Corydorus
Keyhole Maroni	#25 Cichlid, Keyhole

Killie Family - #50

Kisser	#44 Gourami, Kissing
Kisser, Pink	#44 Gourami, Kissing
Kissing Fish	#44 Gourami, Kissing
Kissing Gourami	#44 Gourami, Kissing
Kissing, Green	#44 Gourami, Kissing

Knife, Clown - #51

Knife Fish	#51 Knife, Clown
- or	#52 Knife, Ghost
- or	#53 Knife, Glass

Knife, Ghost - #52

Knife, Glass - #53

Kribensis - #54

Kribs	#54 Kribensis
Kuhli Loach	#59 Loach, Kuhli
Lace Synodontis	#18 Catfish, Synodontis

Leaf Fish - #55

Leeri Gourami	#47 Gourami, Pearl Leeri

Loach, Clown - #56

Loach, Dojo (Weather) - #57

Loach, Horseface - #58

Loach, Kuhli - #59

Loach, Weather (Dojo)	#57 Loach, Dojo (Weather)

Loach, Yo-yo - #60

Loachata	#10 Botias
Malarii	#20 Cichlid, African
Marble	#2 Angelfish
Marble Hatchet	#49 Hatchet Fish
Marigold	#65 Platies

Marigold Wag	#78 Swordtails
Melanistus	#12 Catfish, Corydorus
Melonochromis	#20 Cichlid, African
Metal	#12 Catfish, Corydorus
Mixed Swordtail	#78 Swordtails
Mollies - #61	
Moonlight Gourami	#45 Gourami, Moonlight
Moons	#65 Platies
Mountain Fish	#100 White Cloud Mountain
Neon Tetra	#91 Tetra, Neon
Opaline Gourami	#46 Gourami, Opaline
Ornate Rainbow	#67 Rainbow
Oscar Fish	#26 Cichlid, Oscar
Otocinclus - #62	
Painted Glass Tetra	#87 Tetra
Painted Moon	#65 Platies
Painted Platy	#65 Platies
Painted Swordtail	#78 Swordtails
Paradise Fish - #63	
Parva Cat	#19 Catfish, Whiptail
Pearl Danio	#33 Danio, Pearl
Pearl Gourami	#47 Gourami, Pearl Leeri
Pearl Leeri	#47 Gourami, Pearl Leeri
Pencilfish - #64	
Penguin	#92 Tetra, Penguin
Peter's Elephant Nose	#37 Elephant Nose
Phantom Tetra	#80 Tetra, Black Phantom
Pictus Catfish	#15 Catfish, Pictus
Pimoldella Catfish	#15 Catfish, Pictus
Pineapple Swordtail	#78 Swordtails
Pineapple Wag Swordtail	#78 Swordtails
Platies - #65	
Plecostomus - #66	
Punctatus	#12 Catfish, Corydorus
Purple Tetra	#86 Tetra, Emperor
Rainbow Fish - #67	
Ram - #68	
Raphael Catfish	#16 Catfish, Raphael Rasbora
Rasbora Brilliant - #69	
Rasbora, Harlequin	#70 Rasbora, Heteromorpha
Rasbora, Het.	#70 Rasbora, Heteromorpha
Rasbora, Heteromorpha - #70	
Red Devil	#28 Cichlid, Red Devil
Red Eye Tetra	#93 Tetra, Red Eye

Red Minor	**#95 Tetra, Serpae**
Red Moon	**#65 Platies**
Red Paradise	**#63 Paradise**
Red Platy	**#65 Platies**
Redtail	**#10 Botias**
Red Tux	**#78 Swordtails**
Red Velvet	**#78 Swordtails**
Red Wag Platy	**#65 Platies**
Red Wag Swordtail	**#78 Swordtail**
Ropefish - #71	
Rosy Barb	**#6 Barb, Rosy**
Royal Clown	**#66 Plecostomus**
Royal Blue-eyed	**#66 Plecostomus**
Royal Red-eyed	**#66 Plecostomus**
Rumblefish	**#9 Bettas**
Rummy-Nose	**#94 Tetra, Rummy-Nose**
Scissortail	**#96 Tetra, Scissortail**
Scissortail Rasbora	**#96 Tetra, Scissortail**
Severum	**#30 Cichlid, Severum**
Shark, Bala - #72	
Shark, Black - #73	
Shark, Iridescent - #74	
Shark, Rainbow - #75	
Shark, Red Tail - #76	
Shark, Ruby	**#75 Shark, Rainbow**
Shovelnose	**#17 Catfish, Shovelnose**
Siamese Fighting Fish	**#9 Bettas**
Silver Angelfish	**#2 Angelfish**
Silver Dollar - #77	
Silvertip	**#97 Tetra, Silvertip**
Skunk Botias	**#10 Botias**
Skunk Cat	**#12 Catfish, Corydorus**
Spotted Cat	**#15 Catfish, Pictus**
Spotted Raphael	**#16 Catfish, Raphael**
Striata	**#10 Botias**
Striped Raphael	**#16 Catfish, Raphael**
Sunburst	**#65 Platies**
Swords	**#78 Swordtails**
Swordtails - #78	
Synodontis Angelicus	**#18 Catfish, Synodontis**
Synodontis Brichardi	**#18 Catfish, Synodontis**
Synodontis Catfish	**#18 Catfish, Synodontis**
Tetra, Black Neon - #79	
Tetra, Black Phantom - #80	

Tetra, Black Skirt - #81
Tetra, Bleeding Heart - #82
Tetra, Blind Cave - #83
Tetra, Bloodfin - #84
Tetra, Cardinal - #85
Tetra, Emperor - #86
Tetra, Glass - #87
Tetra, Glowlight - #88
Tetra, Head and Tail Light - #89
Tetra, Lemon - #90
Tetra, Neon - #91
Tetra, Penguin - #92

Tetra, Purple	#86 Tetra, Emperor

Tetra, Red Eye - #93
Tetra, Rummy-Nose - #94
Tetra, Serpae - #95
Tetra, Scissortail - #96
Tetra, Silvertip - #97
Tetra, Von Rio - #98

Tiger Barb	#7 Barb, Tiger
Tiger Fish	#7 Barb, Tiger
Tin Foil Fish	#8 Barb, Tin Foil
Transparent Knife	#53 Knife, Glass
Tux Swordtail, Gold	#78 Swordtails
Tux Swordtail, Red	#78 Swordtails
Two-spot Synodontis	#18 Catfish, Synodontis
Upside-down	#18 Catfish, Synodontis

Variatus - #99

Variegated Guppies	#48 Guppies
Von Rio	#98 Tetra, Von Rio
Wag Platy, Blue	#65 Platies
Wag Platy, Red	#65 Platies
Wag Platy, Sunburst	#65 Platies
Wag Swordtail, Blue	#78 Swordtails
Wag Swordtail, Gold	#78 Swordtails
Wag Swordtail, Marigold	#78 Swordtails
Wag Swordtail, Pineapple	#78 Swordtail
Wag Swordtail, Red	#78 Swordtail
Weather Loach	#57 Loach, Dojo (Weather)

White Cloud Mountain Fish -#100

White Clouds	#100 White Cloud Mountain
Zebra Danio	#34 Danio, Zebra
Zebra Fish	#34 Danio, Zebra
Zebra, Psuedotropheus	#20 Cichlid, African

SUGGESTED GROUPINGS

Here, in FINDER THREE, are eleven groupings suggested for aquarium appeal. Before actually buying a specific fish, I recommend that you check the more detailed description in FINDER ONE for characteristics and peculiarities which will help you decide whether, and how many, you would like to buy.

Group A

3 or more - Neon Tetras (#91)
3 or more - Cardinal Tetras (#85)
3 or more - Rasbora Het.s (#70)
2 or more - Corydorus Catfish species (#12)
2 or more - Kuhli Loaches (#59)
1 - Plecostomus (#66)
2 or more - Guppy species (#48)
3 or more - Hatchet Fish (#49)
3 or more - Glowlight Tetras (#88)

Group B

3 or more - Head & Tail Light Tetras (#89)
3 or more - Red Eyed Tetras (#93)
3 or more - Black Skirt Tetras (#81)
3 or more - Brilliant Rasboras (#69)
3 or more - Glass Tetras (#87)
2 or more - Corydorus Catfish species (#12)
2 or more - Kuhli Loaches (#59)
2 or more - Clown Loaches (#56)
1 - Plecostomus (#66)
3 or more - Glass Knives (#53)

Group C

2 or more - Swordtail species (#78)
2 or more - Platy species (#65)
2 or more - Molly species (#61)
2 or more - Variatus species (#99)
3 or more - Cherry Barbs (#4)
2 or more - Corydorus Catfish species (#12)
2 or more - Kuhli Loaches (#59)
2 or more - Clown Loaches (#56)
1 - Plecostomus (#66)
2 or more - Dojo Weather Loaches (#57)

Group D

3 or more - Tiger Barbs (#7)
3 or more - Tin Foil Barbs (#8)
2 or more - Kissing Gouramis (#44)
2 or more - Blue Gouramis (#39)
2 or more - Gold Gouramis (#43)
2 or more - Pearl Leeri Gouramis (#47)
2 or more - Corydorus Catfish species (#12)
2 or more - Clown Loaches (#56)
2 - Paradise Fish (#63)
3 or more - Zebra Danios (#34)
3 or more - Giant Danios (#32)
3 or more - Pearl Danios (#33)
1 - Red Tail Shark (#76)
or: 1 - Rainbow Shark (#73)

Caution : But only *one* shark per tank.

Group E

3 or more - Brilliant Rasboras (#69)
2 or more - Pearl Leeri Gouramis (#47)
2 - Pictus Catfish (#15)
2 or more - Kissing Gouramis (#44)
2 - Dwarf Gouramis (#40)
2 - Dwarf Flame Gouramis (#41)
3 or more - Rosy Barbs (#6)
3 or more - Rainbow Fish species (#67)
1 or more - Raphael Catfish (#16)
1 or 2* - Ghost Knives (#52)

* 2 preferred

Group F

2 - Blue Gouramis (#49)
2 - Gold Gouramis (#43)
3 or more - Tiger Barbs (#7)
2 - Giant Gouramis (#42)
2 - Opaline Gouramis (#46)
1 or more - Raphael Catfish (#16)
2 or more - Dojo Weather Loaches (#57)
1 or more - Synodontis Catfish species (#18)
2 - Paradise Fish (#63)
3 or more - Rainbow Fish species (#67)
1 - Plecostomus (#66)
1 - Chinese Algae Eater (#1)
3 or more - Giant Danios (#32)
2 - Botia species (#10)
1 - Redtail Shark (#76)
1 - Rainbow Shark (#75)
1 - Black Shark (#73)

Caution: But only *one* shark per tank.

Group G

All these fish are aggressive and territorial so the tank should be set up to afford many territories.

2 - Firemouth Cichlids (#22)
2 - Red Jewel Cichlids (#29)
1 or more - Raphael Catfish (#16)
2 - Pictus Catfish (#15)
2 - Botia species (#10)
2 or more - African Cichlid species (#20)
1 - Chinese Algae Eater (#1)

Caution: If African Cichlids are selected, they should be smaller than the other Cichlids in the tank.

Group H

All these fish will eat whatever will fit in their mouth unless it is fast enough to escape harassment.

3 or more - Tiger Barbs (#7)
1 - Chinese Algae Eater (#1)
3 or more - Tin Foil Barbs (#8)
2 - Blue Gouramis (#49)
2 - Pictus Catfish (#15)
2 - Botia species (#10)
3 or more - Zebra Danios (#34)
3 or more - Giant Danios (#32)
1 - Red Tail Shark (#76)
1 - Black Shark (#73)

Caution: But only *one* shark per tank.

Group I

3 or more - Zebra Danios (#34)
3 or more - Head & Tail Light Tetras (#89)
3 or more - Black Skirt Tetras (#81)
3 or more - Rosy Barbs (#6)
3 or more - Gold Barbs (#5)
2 or more - Corydorus Catfish species (#12)
2 or more - Clown Loaches (#56)
3 or more - Pearl Danios (#33)
1 or 2* - Ghost Knives (#52)
1 - Red Tail Shark (#76)
or: 1 - Rainbow Shark (#75)

Caution: But only *one* shark per tank andit should be small
* 2 preferred

Group J

3 or more - Giant Danios (#32)
3 or more - Tiger Barbs (#7)
3 or more - Black Skirt Tetras (#81)
3 or more - Rosy Barbs (#6)
3 or more - Tin Foil Barbs (#8) - small, 1-2"
2 or more - Corydorus Catfish (#12)
2 or more - Kuhli Loaches (#59)
1 - Plecostomus (66)
1 - Chinese Algae Eater (#1)
2 - Botia species (#10)
3 or more - Rainbow Fish species (#67)
1 - Red Tail Shark (#76)
1 - Rainbow Shark (#75)
1 - Black Shark (#73)

Caution: But only *one* shark per tank and only one of the algae-dependent types (#1 & #66)

Group K

In addition to getting along well together, these fish in Group K will also get along with Group C fish.

3 or more - Brilliant Rasbora (#69)
3 or more - Cherry Barbs (#4)
3 or more - Zebra Danios (#34)
3 or more - Pearl Danios (#33)
1 - Red Tail Shark (#76)
1 - Rainbow Shark (#75)

Caution: But only *one* shark per tank.

Chapter 11

SCHOOL'S OUT

```
(Commencement Address)
```

Welcome to the world of aquaria where the mystery and magic of life under tropical waters comes right into your own home. No one will fail to feel a certain sense of serenity and order when viewing the brilliant colors, the graceful motion, and the fascinating comings and goings of the playful fishes of the Tropics. Sometimes you will find yourself studying the actions of your new friends closely; other times you may be only vaguely aware of their comforting presence; but at all times you will know that they are a welcome enhancement to your everyday existence.

Welcome, also, to the strange world of aquaria! Where nitrosomonas bacteria "eat" ammonia and nitobacter bacteria "eat" nitrites . . . . where bubbles make the world go round . . . . where too much ammonia kills. Welcome to the other side of the "looking" glass.

In exchange for the pleasure that they bring you, your water friends ask very little in care - an occasional sprinkle of food in the water - and, now and then, a little of your time to make certain that their water home remains healthful and clean. It was the purpose of this book to show you how to care for your fish, to explain the choices available in doing it, and to make proper care as quick and easy as possible for you. Along the way, if you were so inclined, you may have picked up a rather comprehensive knowledge of what aquarium life is all about.

In the bays, the tributaries, the rivers and the backwaters of the world - not to mention the oceans and seas, Nature provides for its fish. Nature gives the waters motion. The movings of the waters - waves and ripples and tides - swollen brooks breaking on rocks or running over stones - rainfall pounding on the water - storms and winds roiling lakes and ponds . . . . any and all cause turbulence at water surfaces . . cause air to become entrapped in water, and oxygen from that air to dissolve into the water so that the fish can extract what they need to live.

These same motions of the world's waters are cleansing actions which provide continual change and replenishment in local waters and sweep away impurities before they accumulate. The underwater plant life and algae absorb carbon dioxide and give off oxygen. The fish feed on the plants and on other organisms provided by the waters. The bacteria interact on the life in the water and on each other. The hundreds of chemicals in the waters react with each other in hundreds of ways.

But in a tank of water from the kitchen faucet, things are very different. In your aquarium you have created a small but complete ecological system. As in all ecological and environmental matters, everything seems to affect everything else. When one thing is changed for the better, an unwanted or undesirable change may also result. The health of the fish is affected by light and temperature as well as by the purity, acidity, alkalinity and oxygen content of the water. Heat, light and oxygen make plant life grow. Plants give off oxygen into the water. Fish take in oxygen and give off carbon dioxide. Plants take in carbon dioxide. Decaying food particles and fish waste form harmful bacteria and use up oxygen. Much is happening in that outwardly serene aquarium.

As in all ecological systems, there are trade-offs. The perfect aquarium is a balance that depends upon many factors . . . the size of the tank, kind of fish and their habits, sizes of fish, water surface area, decorations, acidity or alkalinity, water circulation patterns, filter capacity and cleanliness, amount of excess food . . . and it goes on and on. But, be not dismayed; *you* have earned your cap and gown at "School of Fish". You have the knowledge; you can evaluate the risks; you have learned cautious and protective techniques. To your understanding add a little care, and some occasional attention, and your aquarium will be the kind of private world that you - and your beautiful little fish - will *all* be proud of. . . . . And happy fish make happy owners.

Congratulations! . . . Many happy hours! . . . Enjoy your fish! . . .

- Sarah

122

This I call the *Read-What-You-Need Indossary* - a combination index and glossary. It is an all-inclusive reference to the words, terms and subjects in this book.

This "Indossary" can be your initial reference when:

1. you want to locate a subject
2. you want to find the meaning of an aquarium word used in the book
3. when you want a quick explanation of some aspect or process described in the book
4. when you need to make decisions about your aquarium.

The short definitions and explanations are applicable only to usage in this book. They are not necessarily technically precise or complete. They are intended to serve for quick reference, as a sort of short-hand explanation, and as a "mind-jogger". I hope you find the "Indossary" a useful, "reader-friendly" feature.

---

absorbed oxygen: 15
> * oxygen absorbed by the water from air trapped in the water; also called dissolved oxygen

acclimation: 38, 39
> * process of adapting a fish gradually to new waters in a manner which protects fish health

acidity: 17, 18, 19, 54, 55, 56, 57
> * water condition when pH measurers lower than a neutral reading of 7.0

activated carbon: 30, 31, 33
> * porous, absorbent material commonly used as filter media to absorb certain inoraganic pollutants from the water

aeration: 22
> * process of getting air into the water

aerobic bacteria: 10, 29
> * those kinds of bacteria which require oxygen to live

aggression: fish: 48, 49, 50
> * attack upon one fish by another fish

"aging" tank water: 44
> * allowing time for a new tank of water to reach a chemically safe state for aquarium use

air diffuser: 28
> * a device at the end of an air line which distributes the air outflow

air line: 28, 29
> * 3/16 inch diameter flexible plastic tubing carrying air from the pump

airstone: 32, 56
> * a porous device connected to the end of an air line which distributes the air outflow

algae: 34, 122
> * unattractive, but harmless, green or brown vegetation growth; food source for certain kinds of fish

alkalinity: 17, 18, 19, 54, 57
> * water condition when pH measures higher than a neutral 7.0

ammonia,
> * fish waste passed as urine; poisonous to the fish
> effects of: 10, 12
> elimination of: 12, 48, 49, 54, 55, 56, 57
> measurement of: 13, 49, 54, 55, 56, 57

ammonium: 55
> * a different form of fish waste; slightly less toxic than ammonia; occurs in acid waters when pH is lower than 6.8

aquarium tank,
> maintenance: 32
> setting up: 41, 42, 43, 44, 45
> tear-down: 38

bacteria: 10, 25, 26, 27, 33, 54, 121
> * micro-organisms; certain of these feed on ammonia and nitrite

biological filtration: 25, 26, 27, 28, 29, 30, 31
> * elimination of ammonia and nitrites from the water by growing bacteria colonies which consume them

box filter: 30, 31, 32
> * filter system (chiefly mechanical and chemical) which houses the filter media in a separate structure inside the aquarium

bubbles, purpose of: 21, 22, 23

buffering down: 18
> * reducing alkalinity in the water, or making it more acid

buffering up: 19, 53
> * reducing acidity in the water, or making it more alkaline

burns: 16, 47, 48, 50

gravel vacuum: 33
    * gravel cleaning device which operates on syphon principle
heaters: 17, 34, 45
health, fish: 16, 17, 47, 48, 49, 50
ich: 48
    * ichthyophthirius, a fish disease
ichthyophthirius: 48
    * a fish disease
impeller: 22, 32
    * pumping mechanism part in certain water pumps
infections: 17, 48, 49, 50
injury: 47, 48, 50
ion exchange: 25, 27
    * a reversible chemical reaction between a solid and a fluid - used in certain filters to remove impurities
magnetic impeller: 22, 32
    * pumping mechanism part in certain water pumps
maintenance,
    filter & tank: 32
mechanical filtration: 25, 27, 29, 30, 31
    * removal from the water of particles - visible and microscopic
medication: 49
media, filter: 27, 30, 31, 32
    * the material in the filter which effects removal of impurities and also supports the bacteria colonies
mg/l: 11, 12, 54, 55, 56, 57
    * milligrams per liter - used in measuring the concentration of nitrite
mini-tanks: 59, 61
    * small, plastic, filtered tanks, under 5 gallon capacity
nitrate: 12, 34
    * chemical compound which is harmless to fish except in extreme concentrations; also a plant food
nitrification cycle: 11, 12, 13, 57
    * predictable rise and fall of ammonia, nitrite and nitrate in water during critical initial period with start-up fish population
nitrite,
    * chemical compound created by the nitrosomonas bacteria which consume ammonia; poisonous to fish
    effects of: 9, 10, 12
    elimination of: 53, 54, 55, 56, 57
    test readings: 53, 54, 55, 56, 57

"scratching", by fish: 48
* a sign of fish distress characterized by the fish rubbing its body against hard objects in the tank

shock, temperature: 38, 39

slime coat: 16, 50
* the fish's outer covering; equivalent to skin

sodium bicarbonate: 19, 53
* a chemical additive used to "buffer up" or make the water less acid (more alkaline)

sodium biphosphate: 18
* a chemical additive used to "buffer down" or make the water less alkaline (more acid)

sponge filter: 30, 31, 33
* filter system which uses a sponge as its main filtering media

stress: 47, 48, 50
* (1) as a noun - fish distress, anxiety and aberrational behavior, (2) as a verb - to cause such distress, anxiety and aberrational behavior

support plate, gravel: 28, 42
* perforated plate which supports a bed of gravel in an undergravel filter system

tank,
maintenance: 32
setting up: 41, 42, 43, 44, 45
tear-down: 38

temperature, fluctuation: 17, 34, 38, 39

thermometers: 17

thermostats: 17
* devices for automatically controlling temperature to selected pre-set levels

toxicity: 10
* the quality of being harmful, poisonous, destructive or deadly to the fish

toxins: 10
* chemicals that are harmful, destructive or deadly to fish

transferring fish: 37, 38, 39, 45, 55, 56

turbulence: 16, 21
* violent agitation of the water

undergravel filter: 28, 29, 30
* filter system which relies upon a bed of gravel to remove particles and to support the bacteria colonies which eliminate ammonia and nitrite

uplift tube: 29

* rigid vertical tube in undergravel or sponge filter system which carries water from bottom to top of tank

vacuum, gravel: 33

water changes: 33, 37, 38, 39, 53, 54, 55, 56, 57

wet/dry filter: 27, 31

* a sophisticated biological filter system employing both submerged and above-water filters and often incorporating mechanical pre-filters and auxiliary chemical filters

wounds: 47, 48, 50

Zeolite: 30, 32, 33

* an ion exchange agent of aluminum silicate

TANK POPULATION RECORD page _____

Date Added	Fish Name	Qty	Comments

TANK POPULATION RECORD

page _____

Date Added	Fish Name	Qty	Comments

Date Added	Fish Name	Qty	Comments

TANK POPULATION RECORD   page _____

Date Added	Fish Name	Qty	Comments

SEND A FRIEND TO SCHOOL . . .

Enroll now in our "Send-a-Friend" program!

Actually, it's the other way around. Instead of sending a friend to "School". . . you send *School* to a friend. Either way, the idea is that you pay the tuition, and the friend is forever grateful.

If you found Sarah Fell Keppler's *SCHOOL OF FISH* informative and valuable, order a copy of *SCHOOL* for a friend who shares your enthusiasm for fishkeeping. It is a perfect present, also, for someone just now considering a first aquarium.

We'll include a personal note to your friend, signed with a handwritten "Sarah", if you so desire.

SCHOOL OF FISH makes an ideal gift for Christmas or birthday . . . or just because it's always fun to give pleasant surprises to friends.

(Ordering information is on the reverse)

GIFT ORDER INFORMATION

In the year of this printing, we are able to offer gift books through fourth class mail at the following price:

Book	$12.95	per copy
Shipping & handling	1.75	per copy
Total each book =	$14.70	

Should cost increases force a change, orderers will be so advised. Allow up to 3 weeks for fourth class mail.

Please add 5% Sales Tax for books shipped to Massachusetts.

ORDER FORM

(It is not necessary to remove this page; a photocopy—or a reasonable facsimile, *typewritten* or *printed*—containing the same information is acceptable.)

To: Gift Order Offer   Date:_____
PETSPUBS PRESS INC.
Box 2658
South Hamilton, MA 01982

I am enclosing ☐ personal check or ☐ money order payable to PetsPubs Press Inc., in the amount of $_____. Send _____ copy(ies) of Sarah Fell Keppler's *SCHOOL OF FISH* to the address shown below:

Name_____

Address_____

City_____ State_____ Zip_____

(Signed)_____

☐ Check here if you wish a note signed "Sarah" to accompany the book and fill in the following blanks.

Dear _____(friend's first name):

    Our friend, _____(your name), ordered my book for you. We both hope that you enjoy it. Please show it to your fish and watch those fins move in appreciation.

                                        (signed "Sarah")